D1145105

Didier Drogba: The Autobiography

Didier Drogba
THE AUTOBIOGRAPHY

with Hervé Penot

Foreword by José Mourinho

First published in Great Britain in 2008 by
Aurum Press Ltd
7 Greenland Street, London NW1 0ND
www.aurumpress.co.uk

Originally published in French as *Didier Drogba: "C'était pas gagné"* by
SAS L'Equipe & Co./Editions Prolongations

A catalogue record for this book is available from the British Library.

ISBN 978 1 84513 388 7

10 9 8 7 6 5 4 3 2 1
2012 2011 2010 2009 2008

Designed and typeset by SX Composing DTP, Raleigh, Essex
Printed and bound in Great Britain by MPG Books, Bodmin, Cornwall

CONTENTS

FOREWORD

I'm a person who likes to treasure memories, and with them I can tell the world many things. I'm not a writer, even less a poet, but my life has been rich with stories, stories full of extraordinary moments. Looking back at them, I can find only a few special people who I will keep in my soul and in my heart forever.

Didier Drogba came into my life in the fifth minute of a Champions League game in Marseille's mythical Vélodrome. I'd hardly sat down when that giant with the number 11 on his shirt scored. I remember he celebrated that goal like it was his last and he turned an already hostile atmosphere into a fireball of flares, chants and emotion. The crowd went mad, the noise was deafening.

At half-time I found him in the tunnel and told him: 'I don't have the money to buy you, but do you have any cousins that can play like you in the Ivory Coast?' In the middle of this tense qualification game he laughed, hugged me and said: 'One day you'll be in a club which can buy me.'

Six months later I signed for Chelsea. I had found a super powerful club which everybody wanted to negotiate with, everybody wanted to be linked to – and everybody wanted to play for. I had a number of options, but I arrived and said: 'I want Didier Drogba.' Doubts and questions were raised by a few people: 'Why this one?', 'Why not that one?', 'Are you sure he will adapt?', 'Is he really that good?'

'I want Didier Drogba,' I said.

A few days passed and I finally met with Didier in a private airport in London. Again he hugged me, but this time in an unforgettable way: an embrace that showed this man's gratitude, and the affection he feels towards people who mean a lot to him. Indescribable. Then he told me: 'Thank you. I will fight for you. You won't regret it. I will stay loyal to you forever.' And that's just what he's done . . .

His loyalty came out in his leadership and in the way he always faced up to the difficult moments. Moments when nothing else matters than to be there for your leader and your colleagues. This was a person I knew I could count on whenever and wherever I needed. When the team was under pressure he would go back and help the defenders; when he felt pain he would stretch himself to the limit and never give up. Then of course came what he did best: he scored and scored. Those goals brought him titles, amazing awards, but what stays with me are the countless stories we have together.

The FA Cup final at the new Wembley Stadium, 2007. Manchester United: the last game of the season. A lot of people thought this would be my last game in charge of Chelsea. It was a great battle, and then Didier scored in extra-time. The final whistle blew and everybody went mad – apart from two calm individuals. I ran into the dressing room to call my wife. One player avoided the immediate celebrations and followed me down the tunnel. It was Didier, chasing me for a hug. The game was over but in his mind as he left the pitch was only one thing: to hug me as soon as possible. Was he remembering our first encounter? Our second? Or was he thinking that this embrace could be the last . . . ? He found me, we hugged and we cried.

Didier is a special person. And I repeat if I may: *person*. I could say *player* of course – and he's an unbelievable one – but above all, his impact on the world at the moment is as a person: as an African, as an emperor of the Ivory Coast, as a father, as a son and as a friend. And some of us have the privilege to have him in our lives.

Months after the Cup final I was out of Chelsea. As on the first day, there came that same embrace. I couldn't speak and Didier could only say: 'This is not possible, this is not possible, this is not happening.' I could only find the strength to turn and walk away.

Perhaps this preface should focus on Didier the player. But the player everybody knows – the leader, the title collector, the benefactor as well. All these things he has achieved with skill, effort and humility. Didier is in my life as one of the best players I have managed in my career. But much more importantly, he's in my life as one of the best and most unforgettable friends.

Together, the two of us side by side, fighting for the same thing? Far away? In different clubs? In different countries? Or old, with Didier in retirement and me coaching in a wheelchair? It doesn't matter . . .

Didier. Always near to my heart.

José Mourinho

Prologue

IS THIS REALLY ME?

I s this really me?

I came up with this idea on 25 March 2007, in the charged atmosphere of our victory in the African Cup of Nations qualifier in Madagascar. As I got to our hotel, I couldn't stop thinking about my country, at war since 19 September 2002 and finally taking its first steps on the road towards peace. I mentioned my plans to Jacques Anouma, the president of the Ivorian football federation. José Mourinho, the Chelsea coach, gave me an extra two days so I could present my prize for African player of the year in Côte d'Ivoire, the first in the Elephants' history. This reward fed into my plan . . .

There's one thing I can't stop thinking about, like some

kind of itch, and it's when I have to go to Bouaké, the capital of the 'Forces Nouvelles' (New Forces) – the name given to the former rebels – and bring the national team there. Côte d'Ivoire is cut in half, split up by some fictional border between north and south, between two antagonistic camps.

Laurent Gbagbo, the president of the Republic, has just named Guillaume Soro, leader of the former rebellion, prime minister, and this is a significant act that I want to come and support. We football players have long helped in reuniting the country, renewing its overstretched bonds. While the Elephants are fighting, Côte d'Ivoire can bandage its wounds.

I'd promised that I'd come and present my trophy to the head of state and to the Ivorians. All Ivorians. Those of the north, deprived of so much joy for so many years, those of the south who have an easier time supporting us. After I was named African Footballer of the Year in Accra on 1 March, I didn't have time to come back and spend a day in my country due to my professional obligations towards Chelsea.

Since the conflict began, my team, through its results, has played a more and more important part in this quest to make peace, and as the captain I am to some extent the symbol of this as yet unfulfilled hope, a sort of 'facilitator'. People watch my every move, listen to my every word, and I want to make the most of that, help my country to pick itself up off the ground.

I want to believe there's an end to that tunnel; I want to believe in a light that will glow and brighten the years to come.

This gesture isn't a political one; I don't take sides, only that of peace regained.

To my great surprise, these recent years have proved how much my presence seems to impact my fellow countrymen. My words ring louder, their echo reaches further. Too much so at times. I'll come back to that.

I am a guest at the presidency of the republic on that 26 March and I begin to speak, feeling both tense and emotional. I clear my throat, my tone wavering, my nerves on edge.

I ask Laurent Gbagbo if there is any chance we can organise the second leg of the African Cup of Nations qualifier against Madagascar for 3 June in Bouaké, and for me to go to the area said to be under siege to unveil my trophy, the pride of all the nation.

We'd already tried to visit the country from east to west and north to south after the 2006 World Cup, but our elimination during the first round had left us with a bitter taste. It definitely wasn't the right time to start prancing round like heroes.

That match in Bouaké against Madagascar would be the first with the Elephants in years. It would be a symbol. So many problems and dangers lie in the way of this wish . . . I know this, but bringing this city, stuck in the middle, and its inhabitants who have suffered so badly back onto the map of a united Côte d'Ivoire would be a major step towards ending hostilities. Maybe a trigger to break down the barriers of misunderstanding. It's our Berlin Wall. We play and we talk to each other. We play and have fun. We play and get closer. We break the spiral of misery, conflict and outdated 'ethnicity' and we put an end to this pointless war.

This false border would collapse on its own under the influx of supporters from the south. After that politicians would step in to sort out the last hurdle, to hum the anthem of peace. Delighted but anxious, Laurent Gbagbo agrees to the idea of this match like no other. He sees me off to Bouaké with a delegation from the federation on 28 March. 'I'll make a special plane available to you so you can come and go without problems,' the president tells me.

This leap of faith is intriguing; gossip, which is an Ivorian speciality, spreads at the speed of sound. We've heard so much about this town, the armed men who wander around there . . . Still, I feel at ease, serene. Without pretension, I think, 'Who would dare touch me?'

What a shock as we arrive. A cortège of followers is escorting us on the road leading to the centre. I see mothers crying, old men eyeing me up and down . . . I am grasping the impact of my visit; I am no longer a football player, I am an apostle of peace, a bond between the north and the south.

I feel the soldiers' Kalashnikovs brushing me, but no anguish or tension; everything is under control, organised. What is there to fear? I don't feel any risk of things slipping out of control, the crowd is subdued. It takes more than forty minutes instead of ten to reach the headquarters of the Forces Nouvelles where Guillaume Soro is expecting me. The future prime minister welcomes my initiative, thanks me and brings up the subject of the Côte d'Ivoire–Madagascar match taking place in his town: everything will be in place. We set out for the Place du Carnaval. It's more than forty degrees. We wait for an incredibly long time.

On the stage, sweat streams down my body in the stifling heat. There are thousands of people there, cheering me on, wrapping me up in their love. The ceremony is cut short and my speech reduced to two or three sentences. Hands jostle us and reach to grab us . . .

I am promptly extracted from this swell of public feelings, this indescribable madness. My first contact with Bouaké has confirmed my new status: I have become an icon and I can help to ease their pain by being on the pitch. My country is in a bad way. Would I have believed all this as a child, when I left this welcoming land, returning for holidays filled with laughter? Would I have believed this descent into hell, thousands of people dead in pointless combat, child soldiers, millions displaced, this violence dragging such misery in its wake? And me, amid all this pain, making peace, a symbol of reconciliation. After all, I'm just a simple footballer, not some hero.

The country has drawn me in and I accept this. I accept this outpouring of love. Could I even have fathomed not being able to walk down the streets of my childhood, not being able to wander around without causing some unbelievable crush? Could I ever have imagined such a gush of affection, not being able to spend a few days' holiday in the humid tranquillity of Abidjan? One morning as we were coming out of a nightclub, a friend of mine even saw his bumper being ripped off as some kids clung on to his car. His only crime? I'd been spotted by his side.

Nothing prepared me for the frenzied vortex I'm living in. Imagine this scene, like a sign: I am back in my Yopougon neighbourhood, right in the throbbing heart of Abidjan, this African megalopolis, refuge to all hopes. I've just signed my first professional contract with Le Mans. I'm 21 years old. Le Mans, second division, my true beginning in high-level football. As a kid, I used to dream about Marco van Basten, the great Dutch striker, combining power with technique; I move on to Dagui Bakari, my Ivorian friend in Le Mans, hoping to one day reach his level.

In Yop, fresh off the boat, a little smug, I dare to boast about this victory, this professional contract signed on the corner of a table. 'Hey guys, I'm a pro now!' They smirk at me: 'Here's another poser from France.' This annoys me, so I come up with a brilliant idea: I ring up Djibril Cissé, who plays for Auxerre and is already a big star in France. He's from Côte d'Ivoire too. The guys are impressed. Or seem to be . . . Do they really believe that Cissé is on the phone to me or do they think this is some new stunt by Drogba the compulsive liar, never short of something to show off about?

I'm a professional player. A simple professional player who to some seems already to be nearing his limits at 20 years of age. Not always serious, but constantly ambitious.

A few summers later, I am a different man. My life has unfurled like a beautiful novel. Almost like a dream. So there is a God, and he is good, there's no way I can doubt this now. Nothing made me ready to be worshipped this way.

Same neighbourhood in Yop, June 2007. Same street, but this time a wild reception. I bring my friends to this place I left behind so long ago, returning to my past. The house and its walls bring back so many memories. It only takes a few minutes for news of my arrival to spread and the crowd gathers and swells. I get up on the balcony of my family home and see hundreds of people gathered beneath the window. Hundreds? Maybe easily a thousand. Numbers don't even matter. The whole neighbourhood's spread the word. I get out, nosing through the crowd with my 4×4, worried that I'm going to crush the most reckless ones who are holding on to the doors and bonnet of my car. Always this incredible passion.

I find it again on 3 June, the day Côte d'Ivoire plays Madagascar. Madness in Bouaké. Endless queues wrap around the stadium. Our return to Abidjan takes five hours, just long enough to experience this unforgettable welcome. For those people, our presence marks the beginning of the end of the nightmare. Over there, in this overheated stadium filled beyond capacity, soldiers from the regular army have come to cheer us on in their uniforms, right in the midst of their former enemies. This bonding gesture was almost unimaginable just a few days before. As we try to leave, we trail behind the 'compagnie Guépard', the military elite of the Forces Nouvelles. Weapons in hand, they are rough as they open the way, crashing into the reckless with little regard, beeping their horns and shouting as they go. The crowd of die-hard, death-defying fans on mopeds is pushed aside. This welcome is unreal.

Almost two months later, this stadium is to host a bonfire of peace, a political ceremony where Guillaume Soro and Laurent Gbagbo burn weapons in front of some of Africa's most important heads of state. I am proud to think that we contributed to breaking down the tensions and that I have been part of the driving force. Laurent Pokou, a former Ivorian idol, once wrote to me: 'Your most beautiful goal wasn't for Chelsea; it's the one you scored for all the Ivorians you managed to reason with to bring back peace.' This is powerful, deep, moving. I actually wanted to score against Madagascar just to close the loop and I managed it. The final goal, the goal of hope, not that of the victory we'd already easily won. There are goals like these that reach beyond their value in terms of mere sport.

But I draw no merit from it, just the satisfaction of helping my country turn a dark page. I have to make use of my exposure, it's my duty as a man and as an Ivorian. Anyway in my country, after twice passing through Bouaké, I actually heard: 'If Drogba went there, it means the war's over.' I am honoured, though this status sometimes overwhelms me.

On 9 June 2007, my fan club holds a party at the Houphouët-Boigny stadium. About 40,000 people crammed in the stands. Côte d'Ivoire's greatest DJ artists parading on the stage, paying tribute to me, playing their hits to a crowd in a trance. I get on the racetrack that circles the pitch perched on the roof of a car with my wife, Lalla Diakité, who's been by my side through all the fights, who has been so instrumental in my rise to fame. The crowd erupts. All the security and riot police here can't control the rising pressure. Even the car succumbs, with a leaking piston rod.

Some of my friends from the team are by my side in the VIP area; others wanted to be here but schedules don't always coincide. Kolo Touré, from Arsenal, stands right behind me; Abdoulaye Méïté from Bolton, Chico Tiene from Saint-Etienne, Didier Zokora from Tottenham are all close by, faithful.

The fans reach out to me. They're pushed back, often forcefully, by security. Others are dancing on the roof of the decrepit stadium at their own risk. The speaker orders them to come down. No way. I grab the microphone, thank the people for their welcome, feeling incredibly moved. I hum a tune to try and hide my emotion. My teammates join in, all together. On my left, Aubrey Hooks, the US ambassador, busts a move. I'm overcome with happiness. It's almost too much to bear, too huge.

Three days earlier, my mother and father hold a party for me in the west of Côte d'Ivoire, on their own land. An emotional flight in the presidential plane to avoid hours of driving, then a police escort for the last fifty kilometres. A new shock: every village we pass through is expecting me, human road blocks spilling on to the tarmac. Everyone pushing together, blocking our route, wanting to get through to me. The car I'm in has tinted windows but this ruse doesn't work and the policemen have to use force to split the crowd. It doesn't stop all the smiles, or the euphoria they bring.

This ceremony attests to the weight I carry in this area my parents hail from: thousands of people are waiting for me, some of them pushing through the safety cordon, throwing themselves at me. These are images I saw as a child with rock stars, those screams, out-of-control surges . . . One man even falls at my feet and has to be helped up. A manly hug practically cracks my ribs. If José Mourinho, my Portuguese coach, only knew . . .

I grasp the meaning of the messages, of speeches in my name, local truths: I am providing a school in my father's village, helping out in my mother's. I always bring education into my speeches.

Soon it's time to leave again, get back on the road and get on the plane before nightfall, or it'll be impossible to take off from this dim airport. Mission accomplished. During this trip, a teenage boy has given me two notebooks he's dedicated to me. I'm overwhelmed. He wrote all these poems highlighting my career with simple, sometimes childish, always powerful words. He opened up no holds barred, proclaiming his love for me.

His dream was to meet me, to give me these burning declarations. Over the years I became in his heart a substitute for his Guinean father, who died a few years before. A surrogate father . . . How can one come to mean so much to someone, to almost become this fantasy?

Over those few days' travel in Côte d'Ivoire, this month of June 2007, I saw just how much my destiny had changed. To think that in 2002 I was still walking the streets of Abidjan, peaceful and serene, anonymous amongst everyone else. Back then I'd hear the crowds' roars coming from people's homes, my fellow countrymen's pride as they watched the Senegal–France match (1–0) that opened the World Cup in 2002. I had to leave Abidjan, get back to Guingamp. I was getting my plane ticket to Paris . . .

That World Cup now seemed so far in the past. I'd never been selected to wear the Elephants' shirt and my country had never known this stellar competition. You can always dream about it but do you ever really believe it when you're nothing but a simple pawn in a modest Ligue 1 club? Back then I obviously didn't stand a chance to wear France's cockerel, the country whose nationality I also hold. Yet I would one day hear from my agent and older brother Thierno Seydi that Jacques Santini, then les Bleus' coach, had asked him if I was worth selecting. Anyway, I never had to make the choice.

It was such a short while ago . . . Right then I had to go back to Brittany, to a team without any star players. Fight for a starring role. Fight to survive. Fight to succeed. In the end I think I always believed in myself, though of course I never imagined I'd step right into my country's legend. The wheel turns so fast. Faster than you'd expect.

In August 2002 I scored a goal against Lyon as a substitute. It was my birth into the top level; that same month, I got preselected by Jacques Anouma for an expanded team led by

Robert Nouzaret, the start of our epic adventure as the Elephants; on 19 September, war broke out in Côte d'Ivoire. Kind of a summary of my career, a condensed version of an existence that gathered speed and then forked off.

Nothing would ever be the same again for this little expat, the great traveller, the kid with all those cities stamped on the pages of his passport. For a man who's seen it all and might have remained an eternal promise or, who knows, joined the French team alongside Thierry Henry or David Trézéguet.

Everything began with my departure. I was five years old: Michel Goba, my uncle, a professional player and my father's brother in France, was taking me in. That was how it all started. My pains, my happiness. My life as a sportsman. My life as a man.

1

UPROOTED

Leaving, never coming back. Leaving everything behind – my home, my father and mother who I was so close to. An exile is much more than a wrench, it's a stab in the heart. I left the Ivory Coast with a heavy heart, having such a close relationship with my mother, for whom I had always been 'Tito', nicknamed after the famous Marshal and hero of the ex-Yugoslavia, a name which means comrade. Son and comrade. Son and friend. But in the end her son. I can still see my farewell at Félix Houphouët-Boigny airport, named after the first president of the Republic. Quite a dramatic setting for a child who felt his destiny slipping away from him. It didn't take me long to understand. I was only five years old, yet I have an almost perfect recollection of that day. The faces, the bodies, the shapes. And of course my tears. I'll never forget that six-hour journey, punctuated by sobs and short naps. I snuggled in a blanket, clinging to this comforter like a last link with home. You need to have experienced expatriation, even at a less tender age, to understand. The pain, the images, always stay with you.

Leaving your country, your very skin, to seek your future elsewhere – what could be less natural? Most involuntary exiles have experienced the feeling of a rupture in their life, the loneliness, the attempt to forget. But you never forget your roots, you never wipe out your history. It was this fissure that made me the man I am. You don't leave for pleasure (and if there is any, it pales into insignificance), but to seek a better life, a springboard for future generations. This was the hope of Albert and Clotilde, my parents.

In Africa, children are often looked after by the extended family – uncles, aunts, and sometimes more distant relatives. It isn't a matter of getting away from your offspring but rather giving them a chance to grow up in the best conditions. This was, anyway, what my father wished for. Not that we were poor: we had never lacked for anything. My father was a bank employee, and my mother was still a student at the time I flew away. I am the eldest of six children, in fact seven as my father had adopted a street kid of my age, who became like a twin to me. Leaving meant cutting this cord, wrenching me away from such a close friendship.

In Albert's eyes, my future lay in France. He was fatherless, and life had taught him to be strong. From a very young age he had learnt to get by on his own, to help his mother. He built a house and gave her every support. A proud man, he made his own luck, and while he had faced the difficulties of life in the Ivory Coast as a child, he wanted to prepare me and give me the keys to success.

I would get a good education in France and from his brother Michel Goba, a professional footballer over there. Michel was a bit like our 'American uncle'. Picture it: he came back to the Ivory Coast every year, bringing shorts and football shirts. My first shirt was Argentina, a priceless relic I have kept to this day. Even funnier: he brought us new coins from around the world, and we wondered with amazement how they could be so shiny. Anyway, my uncle seemed a kind of distant mystery. He and Frédérique, his Breton wife, would become my 'new' parents, but I was leaving behind me so many everyday pleasures. The clearest was my mother and I sat on the pavement near the BICICI, the name of the main local bank, at le Plateau, the Abidjan business centre, waiting for my father . . . Or going back to nursery school. All those. But I knew that once I left I would be for ever tied to these simple moments.

Soon I would be living my life to the rhythms of Michel's sporting adventures – you only have to read his CV to see what a bohemian, nomadic life I led: Brest, Angoulême, Dunkirk, Abbeville, Tourcoing, Vannes . . . A veritable Tour de France for this young boy from the Ivory Coast, minus the bike. Each season we were off to somewhere new. When I landed in Bordeaux, my first destination on the Continent, I never expected such perpetual motion . . .

And in the end, my French uncle was somebody. I was instinctively proud of him. A professional footballer – that was really something. A nice apartment, enviable social status. I can still remember Angoulême as a kid – the floodlit stadium, the excitement of the match, and then nothing – the void before and after the final whistle. I was instinctively touched by the whole spectacle.

Although I had told my father I was going to be a doctor, I started to feel a certain affinity with the ball. I already had all the equipment and even a classic old-time Saint-Etienne kit. But there was a problem: I was still too young to get a football licence, and I had yet to learn that I was different, that there was a kind of subtle racism in play, or rather ignorance.

You soon learn about this when you come to a place where there are no black people. Sometimes kids rubbed my skin to see if the colour would come off . . . I didn't get it. I myself, apart from my aunt, hadn't seen many white people in the Ivory Coast. Not long afterwards I understood that there was an issue when I saw shutters closing as we passed. I experienced all these strange attitudes which left bitter memories. We were the blacks, the foreigners.

In France I discovered a new life. I had been used to the communal courtyards that connected homes in Abidjan, evenings spent amongst a group of people. The noise of often forceful words resounded through the night, and we would play football barefoot, avoiding holes in the ground. Here, this was impossible. I can't say that I was shocked by modernity – Abidjan in a prosperous Ivory Coast had its share of stylish buildings. Not for nothing was it called 'Little Paris' after the French capital. It was the relationships between people that surprised me, especially as we moved every year for Michel's career.

The hardest thing wasn't leaving my friends but making new ones. Always the same old thing: we moved somewhere and I was the only black in the class, sticking out like a sore thumb. Over time I grew to hate going back to school – the days when we had to line up, present ourselves, with me always the only black kid in the background. For a long time my only friends were the children of other footballers, passing acquaintances. Like Nolwenn Leroy, the winner of *Star Academy* and daughter of Jean-Luc Le Magueresse, a teammate of my uncle at Brest. Over the years I never kept up close relationships with my childhood friends.

But I wasn't destined to stay in France for very long – after going home on holiday at 8 years of age, there I stayed. Michel, I learnt much later, was filling in all the papers necessary to legalise his ward. The political relations he'd gained from his trade came in useful. Support is always important at times like this. I benefited in my own way – unknowingly.

My return to the Ivory Coast took me to Yamoussoukro, where my father had been transferred, and the capital of the Ivory Coast, a hundred kilometres north of Abidjan. Everyone knows its famous basilica, the folly of Félix Houphouët-Boigny. This was a crazy year, surrounded by friends. We were there with Jean-Paul, one of my brothers, and we were the kings of the 2-2 and sometimes 4-4 formation – with me as Maradona, one of my idols alongside van Basten and Weah, and him as Burruchaga, the Argentinian international, and we competed for cups made of cut-off water bottles. Cut-price trophies full of sweets, but reward enough. Trophies born from the fertile imagination of kids playing on the street.

With my cousins and brothers, the opportunities for kids' games were endless. This year in the Ivory Coast was one of the best of my childhood. I blossomed, but it wasn't to last. We often went to feed the crocodiles that President Houphouët-Boigny kept in a swamp near his residence.

There was only one problem: my father, who always kept a beady eye on my school reports, turned out to be much stricter than my uncle. Falling below fifth in my class was enough to get me a whack with a ruler, something I had already got a taste of from my teachers, but I now had to endure from my dad. And this wasn't easy – it was a good test of physical endurance. But this education gave me certain values, respect for others. I wouldn't change a thing. My brothers and sisters would later on get off more lightly – my parents moved with the times, as I often told them.

With my papers sorted, I headed back to France at nine years of age. I loved living with Michel and Frédérique, so this second and decisive departure – getting authorisation from the authorities was like getting blood out of a stone – caused me less pain.

The family had grown with the arrival of Marlène and

Kévin, their two children. This was great at first – I learnt to change beds, do simple everyday things that I found really satisfying.

Above all we continued to roam the country. My worst memory: Tourcoing. Especially in terms of friends.

At school I only had a small circle of friends. Worse, when I was playing football all I heard were comments about the colour of my skin. When you are 13, these words really affect you. I finished the season in team B. In school I was hanging around with the bad kids who nicked scooters, and my name was mentioned in a car theft case. This led to a meeting at the police station with my uncle, one of the scariest moments of my life. Fortunately, the police saw through the story: I had had nothing to do with the case. All the same I would rather have avoided the frightening visit to the police station. What a town – these weren't happy times. Even when training I felt alone, numb with the cold.

And then, on reaching adolescence, I really felt adrift. The arrival of the couple's children had little by little changed my perception of things. I felt neglected.

It hit me hard – no doubt the feeling was selfish, but it was none the less real. I was missing my parents more and more. Hearing Marlène and Kévin saying 'mum and dad' brought all my pain to the surface. I drifted far away – way back into my past, digging up buried pain. One of my only pleasures at that time was the Champions League, which I watched on weekdays nestled in my sofa bed. This is when Olympique de Marseille became part of my life, as if by an enchantment. An unexpected meeting, but one which would be for life. I would always stay with OM. I became the perfect supporter, a fan of Papin, Pelé, Waddle . . .

In the early days of my adolescence there were a thousand questions going through my head – about my future, myself, the desire to be far away. I needed to call my parents, hear their voices. I avoided telling them about my loneliness for fear of worrying them.

My father came to France at the beginning of the 90s, to Paris. The economic crisis in the Ivory Coast, accompanied by student riots, had forced his bank to make cutbacks. There was no choice – he came here to help his family, alone at first but then followed by the whole Drogba clan. At first he lived with cousins, friends, aunts, and this former manager worked as a security guard, a cleaner . . . He would get up at two or three o'clock in the morning, all for us. He had to start from scratch before bringing the family back together again. A real example of solidarity, courage, willpower, without a word of complaint.

My own life was charting uncertain waters. Repeating the fourth grade, all was not well in my head, and I felt uncomfortable in my skin. I became less and less willing to accept reprimands from Frédérique. I just needed to find my niche.

I even started signing school reports in my uncle's name, going against everything I had been taught. I even called an aunt and claimed strange things were happening in the house . . . I wanted to go back to my mother, but that was impossible.

While I was repeating the fourth grade, my father, who had moved to Levallois, a suburb west of Paris, with the family, invited me for the holidays. He was furious and stopped me playing football, full stop. I had come to France to study, not to ruin my future. True, my football wasn't exactly professional: I wasn't going down the route of training centres – the way to fulfilling his dreams. Far from it.

In following Michel, I had nevertheless joined most of his teams and shown some sporting potential. At first a centre back, then a right back and swiftly on to being a forward. I didn't mind being a defender as it meant I could also get involved, take corners and free kicks. There was never any question of this for my uncle – he saw me as an attacker, not a defender, full stop. So he asked one of my first coaches to change my position, even banning me from training when he didn't get what he wanted. An experience that taught him to become more flexible – which he clearly did . . .

I loved football. I immersed myself in it. Just a kid, I imitated my uncle. I borrowed his shin guards, I imitated his professional attitude and unashamedly copied his moves.

In any event, my father's threat was non-negotiable. No more football. There was no question of disobeying. That summer I left Levallois and went to stay with Kriza, a cousin studying law in Poitiers. He had a studio where I tried to sleep while he worked through the night. Somehow we got by.

This year spent alone gave me a chance to discover a variety of different sports. Above all, Kriza restored my work ethic, but on his return to the Ivory Coast, degree in hand, I went back to my parents in Levallois. A long time after leaving the Ivory Coast, the family was back together.

At that time I experienced first-hand the problems facing immigrants – overcrowding, the difficulty of being raised in a closed environment. Our home was compact, to say the least: there were eight of us crammed into ten square metres on the third floor – quite a pad! The tiny bathroom was opposite the front door. The only room held a bed for my parents, their bags at its foot, and a table which could be folded away in the evening so we could lay a rug for the six brothers and sisters to sleep on. And a kitchen in the corner full of the delicious smells of home cooking.

You needed to be a contortionist just to get clean, as even the shower was tight. There was no washing machine, and my mother had to eke out the household expenses to help us get by. Hard. Very hard. Enough to make you crazy, especially when the winter cold meant we had to completely seal the room. Not to mention the noise of the children, my little brothers who didn't go to school. Needless to say, concentrating on my books and homework was impossible.

Thankfully my father let me start playing football again. To tell the truth I could feel myself becoming less and less interested in school. This former good pupil was slipping behind little by little. But football helped me get back on track and, much later, I ended up with a vocational diploma in accounting, the minimum my father demanded.

My efforts meant he didn't interfere in my sporting career. Or at least not much . . .

I was already beset by questions: was education really my way out? Was my father fooling himself? I had seen so many qualified cousins with a good CV and skills desperately seeking a job, having to take on menial work to survive. Football at least wasn't burdened with racial prejudice . . .

Our move the following year, to Antony in the south of Paris, to a larger place that needed renovating – where I took my first steps in wallpapering – marked the end of my grand family tour. My life was taking me in another direction, thanks to Levallois – not the town, but the football club.

I'd gone to a try-out, almost by chance, as we lived close to the stadium. A coach pointed to the under-16 team. 'Go on, let's see what you're made of!' A few minutes later came his verdict, and it was all I had hoped for: 'You'll be coming back tomorrow, but with the A team.' It had started – overnight. In 1993, at 15 years of age.

I'd scored with the B team, but I was good enough for the A. I was tall, keen and sharp. It felt like I could stay in the air for hours . . . Of course this was just an impression, but it was enough to keep me and Gérard Pornin, the under-17s trainer, happy. There was just one problem: our move to Antony had totally changed my bearings and my timetable, and I wasn't able to train more than once a week. I developed an encyclopedic knowledge of public transport schedules, the time it took to walk between Massy station and home. On top of that, there were fewer pitches, the school wasn't great, it was really hot at home . . . My father wanted me to hang up my poor football boots for good. But as time went on, football seemed to be the best way into working life.

After registering at a school in Antony, it became more and more difficult to get to Levallois, especially as my mates from the Baconnets area, where we lived, never understood. They thought I was crazy to travel so far to kick a ball around. I was never going to be a pro, so why go to all the bother? No matter – I quickly got my chores out of the way and caught the RER B (the greater Paris train network), but it didn't stop me occasionally missing my weekly training session if I was grounded. Pornin knew my absences were caused by disappointing school results. He made great sacrifices to pick me up in person sometimes, braving rush-hour traffic jams on the Paris ring road. He must have seen something in me – I was his striker, and at the club they believed in me.

At that time, I got into trouble for hitting McDonald's before Sunday matches. The explanation was simple: between the stadium and the RER station, fast food was the only thing on offer to keep me going.

I should say at this point that we're not talking top-flight football at Levallois: we weren't up-and-coming internationals, more like the fourth division. We were way down. But even without working during the week, I'd managed to get myself selected for the Hauts-de-Seine team.

However, the more time went by, the more my chances shrank of joining a professional team. Henry and Trézéguet were breaking through, and I was playing at Levallois. Yet with a strange certainty that I would become a pro. I always scored when I was played out of my league – wasn't that proof of my talent? Or just of an inflated ego? My father didn't share these feelings at all. One day in Antony he came across a careers form I had filled in. To that eternal question 'What do you want to do when you are older?' I'd put 'professional footballer'. Natural to me, but resulting in a furious father and a torn-up form. 'You think that's a profession?' He had seen what was happening to his brother's career, now on the decline. To him, the main thing was to graduate first of all. I didn't entirely obey him . . .

In any event, in the junior team compliments rained down on me. People talked about Sochaux, but I wasn't interested in the clubs in the east: I was afraid of the cold! I joined the Levallois training centre under the orders of Jacques Loncar, whose deputy was Srebenko Repcic, an ex-pro from Red Star Belgrade, a former top-level striker. I owe him a great deal: technique, my skills in front of goal, my moves. His credo: 'You must live for the goal.' He made me happy to score, forced me to work in front of goal. I wore out videos of Papin and the mighty Pelé. I was desperate to learn alongside him, to move forward, to be on time. Not always easy with the RER . . . His training sessions were my idea of heaven.

But I wanted to try my luck at a higher level – try out, get myself seen. To prove that I existed. I had the idea of sending my CV to every club in Ligue 1, the top French division. I borrowed money for stamps and envelopes from my mother and off I went. The letter box became the focus of my hopes, crushed by repeated rejections, if they bothered to answer at all.

I'd just turned 18, and one day my uncle Michel called me: 'Look, I know a lot of people in Rennes. I've got a friend there, Yves Colleu [future deputy of Paul Le Guen at Lyon, Rangers and Paris]. I'll get you a try-out.' You can imagine how happy I was. I didn't tell Loncar, and of course I bumped into another Levallois guy over there! Fortunately he was also incognito. Michel Le Millinaire was the trainer for the Breton club, with Patrick Rampillon running the training centre. On the first day there were 23 of us competing against each other. There were all sorts – I saw a guy arrive with his guitar, a real funny kid. After two days we were down to two: a guy from Bourges and me.

On the third day I trained with the A team: there was Sylvain Wiltord, Jean-Claude Darcheville, Saliou Lassissi, Marco Grassi, Pandurović . . . incredible. How glad I felt – just imagine, I was playing with Wiltord! I will never forget it – it was just great, especially when Rampillon whispered an aside: 'That was a good pass.'

When I got back to Levallois, Loncar was absolutely furious – he'd received a call from the management of Rennes asking for information on this Drogba guy. My luck was out, my little escapade had been discovered. I answered: 'Coach, I'm not happy at the training centre – I want to leave.' His response: 'You're not leaving here!' When the season finished, I just wanted to quit football, or sign with a small club in Antony just for my love of the game. I told Loncar: 'The travelling is tiring me out – I can't train any more. Plus you blew my big chance.' I was seriously questioning the future of my so-called career: this was my first attack of depression, and the most intense. Like a good psychologist, Loncar assured me that I would have my chance, that he would help me find opportunities. Also my mates asked me to come back and help them out. I accepted.

Loncar soon came good on his promise, and I was sent to try out at Guingamp. Like at Rennes, I was put on the short-list, but after a friendly against Saint-Brieuc, Marc Collat, the trainer, got mad at me. The problem was I'd been ill, with hypoglycaemia. There I was trying to show off my skills and I'd fallen flat on my face!

I couldn't believe it! The next day I rejoined the pros, Coco Michel and co. It went well, but at the end of the match I fractured my metatarsal. I saw my contract slipping away from me.

I had really wanted to go, so this was a real blow. I had known Gérard Gnanhouan there, a fellow Ivorian and goalie, and future teammate.

Then a phone call revived my hopes: Dominique Leclerc, trainer of the Paris Saint-Germain youth team, asked me to visit Camp des Loges, the club's training centre. Me at PSG? Me, a Marseille fan at PSG? I was so proud, so happy to get such an offer, and I hadn't forgotten that Weah had worn their shirt. I bought my Métro ticket from Antony and travelled all the way across Paris. I was a total wide-eyed kid. I passed my medical check, and although my broken toe meant I couldn't show off my skills, I could see they wanted me. The next day I came back with my father, who was clearly impressed by the place, with its body-building equipment in the corner of the room . . . He was in heaven. He left me there to go to an important meeting he couldn't miss, while the officials outbid themselves: 'You'll have an Opel Tigra, seven pairs of Nike shoes.' This was my drug. 'Plus a salary of 7,000 francs [1,100 euros] a month.' At Levallois, all I had been paid were bonuses of around 150 euros.

Too good to be true? Not entirely. An older guy came over and gave me quite a serious talking to: 'You'll be signing with us, but remember you're here on a one-year contract. You need to prove yourself. If you get injured, you can't be sure of being kept on, as we don't carry any baggage.' It made me think. I almost flipped. I was coming from the amateur game, where I trained once a week, sometimes less . . . I wasn't sure how I would deal with the competition. PSG had guys like Rai, Loko, not young kids fresh from the training centre. Where did I fit in? Another important thing: they left me sitting for an eternity, like a nobody, until my backside went numb . . .

The contract was ready, I had my photos taken and slunk off, taking the RER back to Antony where I told my father about this less than glorious occasion. He didn't understand. I kept thinking: 'And what if I'm thrown out after six months?' Then fate played its hand – in the evening I got a call from Marc Westerloppe, the director of the training centre at Le Mans, a team climbing the second division.

– We've heard a lot of good things about you. I've never seen you play, but would you like to try out for us?

– I'm injured, so I can't kick the ball or even put a pair of boots on.

– No problem. Do you want to come and pay us a visit at least? We've got some guys from the Paris area, like Dagui Bakari. We put in the effort and now he's in the A team in D2. We're looking for a player of your calibre.

It was a good speech, more motivating than being left waiting on a chair at Camp des Loges after being given a good warning, so I had no reason to ignore the invitation. The hour on the TGV felt shorter than the journey to Camp des Loges. Westerloppe showed me the town, which was really nice, and the training centre. One good thing about it was that the college was near the stadium.

Dominique Leclerc didn't let it go, however, and called me up. It was my decision. I rode the Métro with a sheet of paper on which I had written two columns: the pros and cons of Le Mans and Paris. At PSG there was the car, but a long list of uncertainties in the cons. At Le Mans, I would be signing for one year, for an identical salary and a lot less uncertainty. I had felt ten times better in the provinces – I had received a wonderful welcome. They had not taken me seriously at PSG, except for Leclerc, who really wanted me.

So, in 1997, at 19 years of age, I joined the training centre at Le Mans with a group of 18 other players. There were two trainee contracts, including mine, which caused a bit of jealousy, especially given my physical limitations at the beginning. There were no problems with my technique, as I was afraid of no one when I got in front of the goal, but I couldn't expect much in other areas. The first time I went jogging in the woods I lasted ten minutes before nearly exploding, while everyone else carried on.

My pulse was off the scale, reaching 190–195 with the least effort: it was hot! Jogging exhausted me, and I finished ten minutes after everyone else. Repeated training put my body under strain. I had to learn how to run – I was out of shape, I got injured: my body wasn't taking it well. My mind was my best friend in my quest for excellence, but I felt my dreams were a long way off. I was being eyed by Le Mans in D2, but I was stuck in training centre 2, the equivalent of the fifth division.

At Levallois I was a young star, a young local hero. At Le Mans I discovered what it was really like to compete with players of my level, who had undergone more and better training. Westerloppe gave me lots of advice, and was strict with me – often with good reason. I took it all from him – he had taken me on blind, without knowing me, without seeing me handle the ball. Respect. I couldn't say the same about the rest . . .

A lot of people boast of having discovered me, mostly tall tales, but we'll get back to that later. At Le Mans I also came across Alain Pascalou, who had picked me for the Departmental '92 under-17 selection. I'd had to turn this chance down faced with the fury of my father. I'd been mucking around and he refused to let me travel. But it had been a big chance for me. 'Dad, please . . .' I didn't go – I didn't want to disrespect him – family was still everything. I cried, I begged, but there was no question of disobeying him. What could I do? Even Pornin was angry at me, but he knew my father, and I wrote him a letter of apology . . .

It was after one week at Le Mans that I bumped into Pascalou: 'Drogba, I'm going to make you work. You're gonna find it hard. You'd better want to be the best or you won't make it.' Nobody spoke to me like that! I was told that he was head of academic affairs, deputy trainer of the A team. But still: 'But how can he speak to me like that? He's arrogant!' When I came across a letter among my things, I realised that he was the manager of the famous '92 selection! He'd never forgotten my not showing up. From the first time we met I thought: 'He's got a real chip on his shoulder about me.' Whenever he spoke to me I froze. It was a kind of repulsion. I understood where he was coming from: looking after my food, making sure I got regular sleep, stopping me going out. He was one of the few people to say what he really thought. But this was a new world for me. It was my first step towards top-flight football – my first big matches, the first time I really felt like a footballer. At last I was at the heart of the profession. Not yet at the top, but still, I was only 20 . . .

2

THE ERA OF ENCOUNTERS

L e Mans. About two hundred kilometres from Paris. For four and a half years, I'd be discovering the footballer's trade; its constraints, which I'd sometimes have to juggle, the toughness. The incredible moments of joy, of fellowship. The outstanding happiness. This stay in the Sarthe region of France was the most important moment in my life. There, I came across every emotion as if I was late in revisiting my forgotten childhood. I was a belated teenager, playing with a newborn reputation – at least in Le Mans and the neighbourhood . . . It hadn't yet gone further. Not to worry. My pride was elsewhere, in the apprenticeship the club had offered me, in the friendships being woven.

I landed there at the same time as five other players coming from different backgrounds: there were the guys from Valencia, Clermont, Tours, another from a village near Nantes and me. Naturally, we spent our time together. I quickly made friends with Johan Liebus, the goalkeeper, and Sebastien Mazerat, at one time my flatmate. We were discovering the pro level, having finally reached its door, and the workload it brought. We were all sweating blood, all of us worked to a frazzle, but we were having fun. And then, I met Kader Seydi. Kader could have succeeded in the profession but a nasty wound to the knee shattered his hopes. The world of football is often cruel.

I'd made friends with some pros who never missed a chance to party. After two weeks at the training centre, I quickly found my room opposite Kader's and near these mates with wallets fatter than mine. This housing estate was my university residence, my student breath of fresh air. I hadn't got as far as the bac (baccalauréat, equivalent of A-levels) but I experienced exactly the same feelings. We were amongst friends. We chased after girls left, right and centre. I was only 19 after all.

I hardly talked about myself. Friend of pros, that makes you a novice. I rubbed shoulders with David Camara, Schumann Bah, Momo Sylla . . . These relationships made me important. Sylla and his 4×4, open-top roof, me, elbow on the door and the latest Nike gear. It was a pose I liked. This new universe also taught me that the easy life would never be my companion. The collection of injuries that went along with my Le Mans journey showed me the difficulties of joining the top level: metatarsus, fibula . . . Each year a serious hold-up. Each year a setback. Each year, bruises.

From the start, I picked my pace. Easy. Always committed at training. Often amateurish outside. One way or another, I was changing all the time.

I used to go to eat lunch in the centre before returning to classes. After the Parisian RER, it was bus time. At the centre, you rubbed shoulders with racers from the Elf motor-sport school put up on another floor. At Le Mans, thanks to the famous 24 Hours, driving remains a good path to a high reputation. What's more, you didn't tease each other badly about women. They had an enormous advantage: they snagged the classy girls because they drove fast racing cars. We were just footballers.

The atmosphere in this welcoming place was really great. That was where I spent my time, it was better than being isolated in my flat where I felt too alone. I was happy that Kader's door faced mine, because at times I faced borderline depression. I finally found out the realities of life. I couldn't rely on parents, on savings. I had to pay rent straightaway. I had bills to cover. I earned between 7,000 and 7,500 francs (1,067 and 1,143 euros) per month and my rent stood at about 2,500 francs (381 euros). Not a big gap if you like clothes, the look. Kader called me Tupac, after the famous rapper, because of my crazy style and my haircut. With a nickname like that I had to look the part, didn't I? It was all happening there. The latest model of shoes at 700 francs

(107 euros), the newest jeans . . . I lived like a king but the king was sometimes bare.

In no time at all, the money vanished, evaporated. The late rent accumulated and the club started to close in on me, to figure me out. In particular, to remove me from the source! It cut off part of my salary to resolve my debt problems and left me just enough to live on. Naturally, the landlord complained. Rightly so . . .

I spent several evenings in candlelight when Électricité de France had the bad idea of turning the power off . . . Another missed bill. I invited friends to eat, even to stay, and all of a sudden they went from having light to pitch black. Nice experience, huh?

I made do with what I had. Without asking myself questions. With 300 (45 euros), 400 (61 euros) or 1,000 francs (152 euros), I coped. I was alone in my duplex apartment, I had no constraints. But I always had willpower: my close family began to lack nothing. I always preferred to give my parents what I had left rather than spend it. Whether at Le Mans or later at Chelsea, this philosophy has always guided me.

I was leading a party lifestyle. The nights we used to have. Especially on Thursdays, student night. I stuck with the stars and my classmates. I'd had the chance to train with the Ligue 2 (French second division) group once or twice and was in my own way a bit big-headed. Or rather I felt like I'd made it . . . in fact, I was out of my depth. I considered Dagui Bakari from the Ivory Coast a model, an idol. He was the big star. Serious too. I watched him with eyes filled with wonder. I sometimes came across him in nightclubs with a tearaway friend of his: Liebus.

A great guy. He'd come to collect me in his red banger of a car. It was the only model in Le Mans. Registered in '37. We came up with a strategy. Once night fell, he would honk and pick me up downstairs. OK, we were ready for the girls. Lucky for us it wasn't Guy Roux in charge of the training centre. Believe me, it would have taken a whole lot of cleverness for the Auxerre manager, the king of spotting, to find us in this jungle we knew by heart. We had our camouflage techniques, even if everybody knew you jumped over the wall . . . You walked ten or twenty minutes, sometimes hidden under thick caps, so as not to be picked out. Each of us picked his route. Neither seen nor known. We always walked some metres apart: if a guy was close, the second had time to avoid him. We were kings of the world, of our own little world. Not even pros. But happy. It was a time of no worries when you looked out for each other.

We'd built a giant loft, like in the famous French reality TV show but without the cameras spying on us. We felt like we were at the centre of it all, spotlights pointed on our little selves. There are worse beliefs.

We were living our adventures – we were a bit irresponsible and self-centred. When you start out in football, the clubs forgive a lot. They accept your bad habits, your missteps. They believe in you, and that eclipses the mistakes. They see you as the future of their team, substitutes for when players are injured. That gives you rights, sometimes without enough responsibilities.

We were learning this essential fact. At Le Mans, our home, nobody refused us entrance to nightclubs. Leaving our loft, the doors closed again. Or rather didn't open any more. Our powers of seduction evaporated. With Kader, we dressed sophisticatedly, for a party at Atlantis, the big black nightclub in Paris. Result: 'You're not regulars, you can't come in.' How was it in Paris, my city, we were treated like foreigners? We took ourselves home to the less trendy spots. People do say that no one is a prophet in his own land. I understood that. Another time, Djibril Cissé, who'd gone in much earlier, never saw us arrive. We'd been stopped at the door.

In Le Mans, I realised my privilege. I played it for all it was worth. It sounds stupid but it's the truth.

Regarding dietary notions, they were totally alien to me. My speciality? Pizza Hut. I knew their telephone number off by heart, I was even entitled to loyalty free gifts. And then there was our little table at Dina's, the African big sister in Le Mans. My fridge was sometimes desperately empty. Or filled with Yop. Not quite the same thing as a meal . . .

In Paris we were regulars at McDonald's and crêperies, especially on Rue Marcadet. Needless to say that at the club, the coaches hardly appreciated my lifestyle. The trainers didn't either. Westerloppe often sounded off at me: 'You wolf down anything!' But he couldn't monitor me all the time, even if some quick research turned up some of my secrets. The coaches assumed my numerous injuries were related to my diet, but they had nothing to do with it. I never had muscular problems despite my difficulty keeping up with the training.

These injuries always happened when I was on top form. I'd be all fuelled up, pushing the machine and . . . bam, fracture. I was in overdrive. My body couldn't handle the workload any more.

The management didn't see it that way, least of all Westerloppe. Just like him to bet on an unknown boy with hardly anybody backing him. I'd left myself wide open more than once for a ticking-off . . .

But bizarrely I trusted my lucky star. Maybe I had moments of doubt towards the end of the first year when I hadn't received the letter confirming I would stay. My situation seemed delicate: I was injured, foot in plaster and on crutches. They weren't sure about keeping me. I heard: is he physically cut out for high-level sport? When a manager talks like that it can be deadly. It shows a lack of teaching ability. I felt like packing it all in.

My fate rested on one detail. My parents had come to visit and I saw my mum's doubts and unspoken questions in the way she looked at me. Fear, almost. I couldn't let them down. Waiting on a bed with a broken ankle: I could imagine better scenarios. In these moments words can soothe you, looks can lend support. I'll never forget the people in the centre, Joël and Bernadette, the cooks, such thoughtfulness, such incredible people. They understood me with my angry look, my broken body and morale. I waited on their comforting words and simple gestures. They knew, felt my passing anguish, inoculated me with their joy.

Since they were outsiders, you knew there wasn't an inkling of jealousy, of competition. I could open up to them, speak from the heart. 'Don't worry. You'll see, you'll get there,' Joël slipped in, under such a sincere smile.

Westerloppe too, in his own way, always gave me words of reassurance: 'Don't worry, we're going to keep you,' he encouraged me at the end of this first year. More proof of his attachment to me. People have told me since that he used to get really angry about me and that Alain Pascalou had pushed him to keep me on . . . Perhaps.

On my side were my talent and my physique. My build was like Bakari's, who was set to leave Le Mans. I watched those guys go, watched their dreams fall by the roadside. I could have joined the reject bin. Without a certain level of achievement, a blind belief in my abilities, certain knowledge that I'd make it and reach great heights. Without the support of Westerloppe.

He'd asked me, when I arrived, 'What are your strong and weak points?' My strong points were my headers, my moves, my scoring instinct. My weaknesses: my endurance, my concentration and consistency. These questions pushed me to know myself better, to learn to examine and question myself.

One more sign seemed positive. Westerloppe had been promoted to trainer of the Ligue 2 team in November 1997, replacing Slavo Muslin, fired after a run of poor results. This change confirmed what I was thinking: how could I not get my chance after everything that had brought me here? Was I assuming too much?

I was persuaded that if I worked at training, which I always did, if I continued to score, he would back me. He had to wait a long time. A very long time. My life off the pitch went off the rails and didn't match the club's image. For a while he didn't speak to me at all. He cut me off. This coldness must have pushed me to react. When I think back to it, I could have wasted everything. I had a chance, this chance to find the needle in the haystack.

I finally discovered the professional game at the age of 21, on 22 May 1999 against Cannes. Albeit late. Before, my career had gone along at CFA2 level, the French fifth division, travelling all over, with makeshift playing fields in unknown towns. I was so far from Trézéguet, Henry, world champions in the magnificent summer of 1998, stars shining already. To me this survival match against Cannes (1–0) was like a World Cup final. Am I exaggerating? Maybe a little.

When Westerloppe told me his intention to add me to the group I exploded inside. My name at last among the greats. My reward. It was Bakari's last match and I had picked up shirt number 33 with no name behind.

At Beauvais, the following match, which we lost, I was still on top form. Two appearances with the pros. One hour in total. Meagre prize list but so gratifying. I felt ready to catch up.

Some days later, I signed my first pro contract under the guidance of Pape Diouf. Yes, Diouf, the agent of Desailly and other stars. And Drogba? You may well ask. I must have been his least likely player to reach the stars. He had, however, gambled on me. I have to credit this marvellous union to Thierno Seydi, Kader's brother, who worked with the actual Marseille president. He had already picked me out on the Levallois pitches, then took an interest in my journey to Le Mans via his brother. Enough to push Diouf to sign a contract. My mates joked: 'What are you going to do with him? He has loads of players, great ones, whereas you're nothing. You don't need an agent at your level.' Too bad. I was honoured to have somebody to represent my rights, especially this agent the whole world was talking about. Even more so as he'd taken me into his team while I had a broken ankle, a fractured fibula and a dislocated knee.

Thierno had been persuasive. He had merit. He was constantly interested in my performances. The first discussions with Pape had been clear: 'I am telling you, just because I don't call you every day doesn't mean I'm not thinking about you. You should even be worried if I do that. That would prove I'm not taking care of you.' Thierno then became a big brother, a confidant. My right-hand man, always there, capable of spending hours on the phone with me. Before a match, after a match.

I didn't need to speak to Pape. Each time an agent tried to sign me up, I would call Thierno: he knew everything that was going on. I didn't want confusion, people claiming to speak in my name. Nothing must spoil this new relationship. I had the best agent: what more could you dream of?

My contract in the bag, decent pay, I was expecting every-thing to fall into place the following year. Time to show Le

Mans what I could do! My first two appearances in L2 had given me a healthy appetite, and I waited for the 1999–2000 season with great impatience. How would I fit into the group? I felt I could scrape a full place, I saw myself as the boy who was moving up. I wore my socks like Sonny Anderson, my collar like Eric Cantona: this slightly flamboyant style was basically a kind of insouciance. We were stars. Aside from basketball, football was the only sport played profesionally at Le Mans. I'd just taken an important first step, but I wasn't there yet. My first matches displayed my growing ability.

On 17 August at Caen (1–1), I went on half an hour from the end. In injury time, the referee whistled for a penalty. We were behind and no one wanted to take it. I took the ball, me, the kid, I dashed forward and scored. My explosion of joy was shortlived: the referee explained he hadn't whistled! Hard blow. David Camara came to see me, encouraged me: 'Don't worry. Stay calm, catch your breath. You'll score.' Nice one. My first professional goal. Almost on the next play, Caen won a penalty. I was mad. I told myself: 'Shit, I really wanted my goal to mean something.' As if a symbol, the Caen player misfired. I won a point for Le Mans. It wasn't a big thing but in my eyes that penalty was when I joined the big boys.

Without a break, Oliver Pickeu, our main striker, was injured and I took his place up front. I was put in the line-up against Cannes and I scored my first double with two headers, one in each half (2–1). I was euphoric. In the anonymity of Ligue 2 the media discovered a young man in dreadlocks. I watched myself on *D2 Max*, a TV show on Canal+ which showed highlights of our championship. What an honour! The family didn't even consider missing the show. It was the first time I saw myself as the big act, and the first time my opponents did.

The weekend after, we travelled to Valence. At Le Mans, Stéphane Samson and I were the men on form. I realised very quickly that we brought a bit of a reputation with us. After ten minutes, I got kneed in the thigh. I passed out. I saw stars. I was literally paralysed. Bye-bye Valence. I was forced to leave my friends. I became prey for my rivals.

I was knocked off my cloud nine. I understood this law of professional football: just as I felt myself moving forward, I got slowed back down.

But this first professional season had fulfilled me in terms of time played and adversity overcome. I took on the hard knocks and rough challenges. I was all set for the second year, which was looking thrilling. As before, I started with Stéphane Samson in attack. My partner wouldn't have me at his side for long. I was injured in a pre-season match against Le Havre where Souleymane Diawara, Chimbonda, Vencel and Caveglia were coming into their game. New fibula fracture. I was devastated – my big opportunity was snatched away. As usual. I had to start over from scratch. Surgery, rehabilitation – the same old hellish cycle. Then set out again. I questioned my seemingly fragile body which was having such trouble adjusting. What if the coaches were right? I was used to being at Levallois, with its weekly training: it was tough to compete with the hard men of Ligue 2.

As I dragged along my new injury like a ball and chain, I saw the team sinking and Westerloppe losing control. I started the rehabilitation seriously. Too late to get my trainer back.

The management had chosen to let him go. It struck me like another blow – I was attached to this man who had taken me on without supervising me, who trusted me sight unseen even if I had lost time because of the crap I went through. Westerloppe is one of the only people who can tell me to my face what he wants: I accept it. You must never forget the people from the start of your adventure, of your rise.

His departure, obviously, badly unsettled me; the more so as Thierry Goudet, his replacement, brought Daniel Cousin with him to make up for my injury. Somewhere along the line, people ignored me. I became a ghost, an intrusive shadow. I no longer existed in their eyes.

Goudet made sure to put me in my place: 'Is that you, Drogba? I'm warning you, you're going to have to get serious because with me it's not like with the other trainers, I work differently . . .' That kind of insufferable stuff. From then on, this remark got in my way. He was telling me I had a bad reputation. But my bullshit was outside football, I had always been serious on the pitch.

I was judged and found wanting with no chance to defend myself. It was tough. I'd lost my appetite for the game, because human relationships were so essential to my progress. To make matters worse, I was having trouble coming back from my injury. But even now Westerloppe helped me and advised me.

I called him, he pushed me to pull myself together. My mentor had put me back on the right track. I trained flat-out; I was still the best striker but I kept being made Cousin's substitute.

The situation weighed on me. Cousin was scoring and he was the coach's favourite. There was no jealousy between us because we were close and I was happy to see him succeed. I just wanted to succeed with him. Goudet obviously didn't feel the same. It was hard because he wasn't giving me a fair chance.

In his motivation speeches he talked about the need to get stuck in. But how do you perform when you're stuck in a tracksuit on the substitutes' bench? I wanted to flex my muscles, tangle with the opposition . . .

Then, Goudet straight out decided to do without me. We were at the end of the season, looking to stay up. I'd always kept my place in the group. I only lost it when I was injured and then I went down on the bench, in CFA2, if I hadn't argued with the pros throughout half-time. You wouldn't have noticed, but my years at Le Mans had given me a little status amongst the guys and I had a whole gang of mates in this team: Olivier Thomert, Frédéric Thomas, Yohan Hautcoeur, Laurent Bonnart and Yoann Pelé, who got involved himself sometimes. Somehow, I was a little like their leader; I took the floor in the group, I protected them. They were my boys.

One day, then, at the end of the season, Goudet dropped me, even from the bench. This moment will never be erased from my memory. For the one and only time, I cried with rage at training. Tears streamed down my face, I was so upset with him. Such rage, I'm telling you, as I never felt again in my life. These tears carried with them some sort of spite, and despair. It was a surreal scene: my friends consoled me. Fred Thomas, Cousin, Bonnart . . . My reaction was instinctive: 'It's nothing guys. I want to leave.' End of story. This anger stayed buried. I didn't accept it. Impossible. Too hard. Behind my calm, peaceful, stoic face there were feelings hiding which could be abused.

Goudet had simply pushed me to a bad place. Rubbed salt in the wound. Each time I went home, I was distressed. Fortunately, Lalla, my wife, was waiting for me with the children. They were my lifesavers. I didn't even want to return to training any more, I found excuses. This was the sign that my leaving was inevitable. People were no longer giving me a chance and I didn't know if this decision was serious or passing. My career was stuck, at 23 years old. I was no longer the big thing at Le Mans in Ligue 2, but a substitute who doubted his own future. Almost the substitute for a substitute.

Fortunately, every year, in May, the Ligue and the national union of professional footballers meet in Paris for an awards ceremony which recognises the best players of the season. At this time, most of the participants at the banquet came from L2. There, in the rooms of a grand hotel in the capital, I met Dagui Bakari and above all 「 ald Ray, a former Le Mans player. Ray was a tremendo nted striker. He asked me questions about my career:

– What's going on with you

– I've been injured.

– Listen Didier, with the skill you have, with your build, you shouldn't get put off. In training, you were one of the best strikers. Be serious for six months because I know you mess about. You'll see, it will pay off. If it doesn't, we'll speak about it again.

Does this monologue seem mild? It possibly changed my destiny. Certainly my career. I'd come to this party to have a good time in Paris, to have fun – which I did – and I left for Le Mans with this leitmotif in my head. 'Be serious for six months.' The phrase came like a kick in the pants – I kept hearing it in my mind. Ray, who seemed a perfect striker to me, had become the ideal advisor.

I went off on holiday with these words in my mind. They bucked me up. I knew the club's intentions though: it wanted to transfer me to the Belgian or Dutch championship. This was pie in the sky. I obviously didn't want to go there. I proceeded as if nothing was up, as if I hadn't heard the rumour. I preferred to remind myself of this phrase over and over: 'Be serious for six months.'

My preparation worked wonders. The physical troubles fell away, and I felt ten times as motivated. I was in a great mental place; unfortunately the coach didn't see any of this. He didn't appreciate me. Problem: every time I went on, I scored. And some of those goals I lashed in during televised matches. That's not to be sneezed at: the clubs see you, the public supports you, your reputation grows.

The club offered me a contract extension anyway: I was able to go from 20,000 (3,050 euros) to 40,000 francs (6,100 euros) per month. In the off-season, the management had already repeated to me: 'You are the future of the club.' Except for Goudet. When 'the future' regularly has his buttocks glued to the substitutes' bench, there's a problem. At the end of December of that year, 2001, we met Saint-Etienne, a Ligue 2 battle at the time, on Eurosport.

I was still a substitute. In eleven minutes, I recorded two headed goals. I didn't know then that they'd be my last in a Le Mans shirt.

The winter break came up and I received a phone call from Laurent Schmitt, nowadays Yohann Gourcuff's agent, a Guingamp staff member. 'Didier, this is it, we're interested in you and we'd like to welcome you. Would you be ready to come?'

'Is this a joke?' Me the Le Mans substitute in Ligue 2 courted by a top-level club? Incredible. Thank you Reginald . . . A few days later Ali Bouafia, sporting director at Guingamp, got in touch. I couldn't believe it. I called out to my wife, who was already at my side. 'It's Bouafia on the phone!' She didn't know who he was, but I was so excited that she understood something important was unwinding. Guingamp wanted me! Almost 24 years old, was I at last going to enter the French elite, which had always shut me out?

Guy Lacombe, the trainer, contacted me next, confirming the club's desire to buy me as soon as possible. Problem: we were nearing the end of the transfer period. Unfortunately, I couldn't get in touch with Thierno, who'd left with Pape Diouf to join the Senegal team in Mali for the African Cup of

Nations. His mobile phone wasn't working, and I couldn't waste any more time. Where to go from here? I had an idea: I decided to call my friend Gourville at Sedan to get Salif Diao's number, a hero of the Lions of Teranga and an Ardennes player like him. Another ploy: I contacted my Malian father-in-law to ask him to find the Senegal team's hotel. I reckoned approaching from all angles would multiply my chances.

Finally I got hold of Diao, who was with Bruno Metsu, his selector, who he passed to me: 'Mr Metsu, my name is Didier Drogba, I'm trying to reach Thierno, it's very important.' Thierno took the handset: 'What is it my son?'

'A club wants me but it needs to be fast, otherwise I won't be able to go there. Thierno, I want to leave here. Quickly. I can't take it here any more. Things aren't working out with Goudet, I don't belong with him. This could be my chance for a rise.' I couldn't stay where I was. It was time to thrive, to liberate myself. I started a sort of arm-wrestling with the Le Mans management. Not really my style but necessary in this situation. The president met with me: I told him Guingamp's offer. 'It's nothing, go home. You'll be forgotten about tomorrow,' he told me.

How could he imagine that happening? Did he think I was incapable of seeing through my ideas? Goudet was the same old Goudet. 'So you want to leave? Don't forget that here, I decide. And I set the price: it would be 3 million francs [457,000 euros]!' Three million for a player who finishes his contract in June and who's polishing the bench. I called Pape and filled him in. 'Guingamp are playing at Metz in four days: they need me.' He did his utmost from his side; I went back to see the president and I gave him an ultimatum. 'President, I won't come back if I can't leave.' I was prepared to stop my career for four months, come what may. At that point Le Mans started taking me seriously. The machine started rolling and the two clubs agreed on a sum of around a million francs. Not three as shockingly demanded. The president said to me: 'But what are you going to do at Guingamp? They're going down!' I was all fired up: 'But the year after, they'll come back while you go down.' A silly thing to say in the heat of the moment.

My mates were happy for me. They encouraged me. We all dreamed of Ligue 1. Goudet was no longer resisting and distrustful. I quickly agreed on the salary with Guingamp. Lalla then had to take me to Brittany as fast as possible: the Metz game was imminent.

I wanted to say goodbye to my teammates, to all my friends who I'd shared so many things with. Four years in a club leaves a mark on a guy's life. But Goudet banned me from the locker room. This attitude hurt me. He warned me: 'You'll be collecting your things this evening.' Thomert opened the door of the centre to me, it was just us. It was a sad end. Not one of those happy endings you see in films at the cinema. I felt like a thief escaping. I had to come back to say goodbye. An anonymous departure would have been unlucky for my career. I had to hear my friends wish me good luck. It's important to me, almost a question of principle, and one that I've stuck to since then.

Goudet certainly had his reasons. He never found the words to drag out the best from me. I didn't appreciate being the expensive last resort he seemed to regard me as. What was behind this abstract notion? I saw only one explanation: in his eyes I didn't have what it took. Full stop.

Some of his actions were also really pushing it, one of which will always remain a true professional mistake. My wife had just given birth to Isaac. Since we were playing in Brittany, not far from the clinic where Lalla was, I asked permission to stay after the match to go back to the hospital. Refused. On the journey back, the trainer tells us that he's allowing us two days off. This was hard to swallow. Some time later, an old team-mate told me how Goudet had explained to him that he was the root of my success. He alone had enabled me to strengthen myself mentally . . .

Soon I'd be discovering Ligue 1 after a useful journey through Le Mans. I'd got the hang of things there and above all I'd found a new stability. This was going to change my life, most certainly. Two events forced me to wake up, to start questioning. I also needed to learn that life in this loft wasn't everything.

The end of my first professional year left permanent marks. We formed a group of blacks with Dominique Gourville, Parfait Medo-Otye, Momo Sylla, who later became my son's godfather. It worked out great . . . We spent all our spare time together, it was a time of sheer friendship. And then, at the end of the year, it was like a flight of sparrows: everybody left.

I was alone again, the hassles began, I broke my shinbone . . . I felt alone, very alone and I realised the limits of friendship when it came to career management. Everyone has his own destiny and can shape it. I needed to think about me. I took time to understand this, to digest it. It's a bit like the end of summer camp when the goodbyes are heart-rending, when you feel you can't ever leave. Even though you've got to grow up and look after yourself.

To get back on track, there's nothing better than a wife. Meeting Lalla Diakité radically changed me. Not just emotionally. Without her, I wouldn't be at this level today. Who knows? Maybe I would have matured but it certainly would have been later.

The memory of our first meeting is still vivid. I was lying down on a settee in my uncle's shop in Vannes. I was helping out in his grocery store at the end of the school holidays. I was 17. Suddenly, an apparition. I saw her, graceful, beautiful. She was with Viviane, my cousin, who was visiting us. She was a little older than me. I fell madly in love with her, I wrote her fiery love letters that I sprayed with my cologne. What passion. I chased after her for a long time after but I was too young . . . At Le Mans, I still tried and the trigger occurred on a visit from Lalla, Kévin, her son, and Viviane to my flat in Sarthe.

She was living in Vannes and the railway line that carried me to this corner of Brittany soon held no secrets for me. Neither did the inspectors. We knew each other, we greeted each other. They no longer needed to look at my ticket. Good news: I didn't always have one.

This period coincided with good times in my football. She turned out to have a positive influence. I was ecstatic, I would take the train right after training, towards Vannes. I'd spend my afternoon with her and leave around 5 or 6 the following morning, so as not to miss the training sessions. If ever there was proof of love . . .

Even though I didn't always have the money during this period, I tried to impress her. Dressed top of the range, worked on my style. She turned away from it: 'What are you doing? You're always buying new clothes. Be careful.'

'Don't worry.' She had good reason to worry though. My spending was getting my finances into trouble . . . I risked everything. One Valentine's Day, I offered her a present at the restaurant that she didn't dare unwrap in front of everybody. She had it tucked away in her bag. Out of etiquette. But I forced her to open it in front of me. All the same . . .

We moved in together in Le Mans in January 2001. Three months later, she was pregnant. I longed for it. Nothing more beautiful could happen. Kévin was here already, her first child, born in 1992. Isaac arrived at the end of the year, in December. An immense joy. This changed my way of life, helped me not to get too distracted any more. Iman would come, later, on 12 March 2003. Another huge family event. I really wanted her to be born on the 11th, like me in 1978, but the day she was due, she turned round! Missed it. By just one day. I was gutted. But I'm not grumbling about this minor nuisance. Without them, I wouldn't be where I am. They are my comfort, my cocoon, my stability. Their happiness comes before everything.

Then, the day I signed for Guingamp, all four of us left and spent one night in the railway station hotel. That's where I had stayed during my youth trial. Four in one room, Iman not having been born yet, of course. My feet were touching the end of the bed. But don't think that meant Guingamp was already too small for me: quite the opposite. Ligue 1 unlocked my ambitions. I already believed in myself, I had reason to. I was joining the greats of my world, with a broad smile on my lips.

3

LIGUE 1 AGED 24

I entered the world of negotiation when I turned up at Guingamp. Pape Diouf had left me with instructions on how to argue. 'Son, give me a call if you have a problem,' he'd whispered to me. He didn't need to be there since everything seemed in place. So there I was in Alain Aubert's office, Guingamp's chairman. I studied the proposed contract, I stopped at the key points but I didn't see the bonus.

I called Pape: 'It's about the bonus, I don't see anything. Has there been a problem?' 'Don't worry, pass me to the chairman.'

Their conversation didn't drag on. Aubert hung up.

'I don't know what Pape Diouf said, but he knows what he's doing.' Everything was in order. I was proud of my dealings. I had salvaged my bonus; I could spend my first night alone at the hotel, finally feeling at home at Guingamp. In Brittany no less. In the morning, Guy Lacombe, the coach, picked me up in his car and dropped me off at training. He started to sound me out, encourage me. 'You're glad you signed, right? You're playing tomorrow. Are you ready?' My response was ready, my body slightly less. 'First game, yes. No problem.' I wasn't trained though. I'd spent my last days at Le Mans soft-pedalling. I knew that I was replacing Fabrice Fiorèse, the local hero, who'd left for Paris Saint-Germain. It was another difficulty, a big obstacle to overcome. I inherited his number 11 and it wasn't easy to take on. I heard the sniggering: 'That's Drogba Tébily Didier? He's never done anything and he's coming to replace Fiorèse.' In some people's view, I was coming out of nowhere and my older age wasn't encouraging confidence in the recruit. Lacombe, at least, was enthusiastic.

At my first session I recognised some friendly faces, people I'd met in Ligue 2 or at my try-out for Guingamp, years before. There was Florent Malouda who I'd met with Le Mans against Châteauroux, a team that suited me fine. I often scored against them even if it rarely led to a victory. Flo took my mind back . . . There was also Gérard Gnanhouan. Blaise Kouassi, a close friend of Florent, was going to turn up later from the African Cup of Nations, which he was competing in on the Côte d'Ivoire side in Mali.

In the locker room, inevitably, I wasn't too sure of myself. I was surrounded by certified professionals. Maybe to put me more at ease, the directors had placed me between Hubert Fournier and Coco Michel, the two main men. Coco addressed me, just to relax the pressure: 'Don't worry, it'll be fine. We have confidence in you.' I realised that in D2 the guys gave each other more hassle, put on airs. Here, the blokes were really incredible. I was able to go to Metz for my first match in Ligue 1. A date not to forget: 30 January 2002. More than a month before my twenty-fourth birthday. I knew the Metz guys by name; I was tracking the club's progress carefully. In those moments you avoid dwelling on doubts, paying attention to anxieties. Maybe it's fear of not appearing strong enough.

Flo helped me the most because he was close to me on the pitch. As this was my baptism in L1, I went at it like a bull at a gate. I ran in every direction to show myself, to prove to Guy Lacombe that he'd made a good choice. It's not always the best way to shine . . . Flo was constantly talking to me, giving me good advice. Above all he wanted me to avoid burning myself out too fast by standing in for me at times. Good attitude. 'Go over there instead, don't run too much. I'm going to do it for you.' It showed he was a great guy. At half-time we were a goal down; I was exhausted. Guy Lacombe spoke to me: 'Didier, you need to give more.' What more could I give? I was running all over the shop! Deep down inside, I said to myself: 'If only you knew, I'm flat out already . . .'

However, I equalised at the start of the second half. We won (4–2) in Gilbert Gress's debut at Metz. The article in *L'Equipe* newspaper talked about a 'Drogba festival for his start in Ligue 1,' and gave me the highest mark along with Saci (6.5). I could have scored twice but I fell as I ran for a deep pass. Stopped dead. I held my thigh, fearful of an injury. Luckily it was only an enormous cramp, but I couldn't go on playing and was substituted.

Somewhere in the corridor, I heard a well-known television journalist say: 'There's Bakari with this Drogba. He's big, strong.' I was honoured. Honoured to have Lacombe's confidence. The trainer had left Cédric Bardon on the bench, the best striker on the team. The Ligue 2 substitute took the place of the biggest hot shot in L1. Empowered by this confidence, I had to go for it, get stuck in. Give everything. Lacombe had saved my skin. This didn't stop him from having a go at me.

Two months after my arrival, his judgment was merciless: 'I am disappointed by your performances, Didier. You are not doing enough on the pitch.' He was using a gem of a psychological weapon. He had aggravated me, I got all fired up. I replied: 'I don't agree. But I'll try harder.' He knew how to take me. He taught me an enormous amount about space and movement.

Tactically, he was dynamite. You wanted to listen to a trainer of his calibre, you couldn't help learning from him. You just couldn't be stubborn, you had to be able to keep perspective when his voice erupted . . . These early stages were hard nevertheless. I was finishing my matches with a last powerful effort through lack of training. I was relieved when the final whistle came – so tired and run-down. I especially remember a home defeat against Paris Saint-Germain in March (1–0). The next day we lost to Montpellier (2–1): I scored the first goal but it wasn't enough. I missed chances then made a mistake marking one of their strikers.

Soon after I received a letter at home. 'Go back to your country, banana eater . . .' This attack almost made me cry. I didn't need this extra motivation, but I'll never thank the author enough. This insult spurred me on. I wanted to prove that you could eat bananas and succeed away from your country. I had been confronted with racism but I never really suffered from it. I put it down more to ignorance and closed-mindedness. It wouldn't surprise me for that matter if this person started to follow me and became one of my fans. If I have, at least, been able to change his mind about Africans . . .

Anyway, in five months, I only scored three goals but I felt I had a chance to make my mark in this championship. It seemed less hard to me than Ligue 2, more suited to my qualities. It wasn't easy though since we were struggling against relegation. Not going down was our obsession. Every-one saved themselves for the last day on 4 May against Troyes (1–0). Unforgettable. At those times the pre-match ritual takes a new turn: sleep doesn't come easily. Images buzz around in your head because the future is waiting. Not just ours. You think about those people who work voluntarily at the club, who dedicate themselves. We didn't have the right to let them down. Some, at the end of their contract, are also contem-plating unemployment. You get the impression of time stopping. You look back on the matches lost stupidly, the points dropped through beginner's mistakes, the goals you missed by a fraction . . .

The pressure was enormous. So was the celebration on the pitch. I finished up in my underpants, we'd saved Guingamp. We were champions of the world. And then, Lacombe announced he was leaving for Sochaux. What a blow. He couldn't do that to me! Just before leaving, he came to see us, Flo and me. 'If you don't mess around, you'll skyrocket. You are the best strikers in France.' I wasn't coming up with great performances though. I told myself: 'He's a great guy, but he's clearing off!' Lacombe, this incredible trainer who loved us.

Malouda and I were inseparable, the Guyanese and the Ivorian. The connection we had never broke. The third man in our association, which was the name we gave ourselves, was Blaise Kouassi. Our trio was certainly tight. We had a crazy time together. Our wives too. They had formed a trade union, and their main issues had to do with our frequent nights out. Danger ahead! They made all sorts of demands: family life, living as a couple . . . We men were forced to stick together. Each of us came to the aid of the others with easy jokes. As on the pitch, one for all and all for one. With Blaise, we tried everything to attract Flo to the Ivory Coast team. He still hadn't put on the blue shirt and it would have been easy to find an ancestor in Abidjan . . .

These first six months in Ligue 1 had confirmed for me that I could make it. I was staying on to see how the following season went without Guy Lacombe.

Bertrand Marchand replaced him. From an automatic pick, I became a part-timer. A substitute guy, in fact. Just after he arrived, Marchand, who's since led Tunisia's Etoile du Sahel club to win the African Champions League, gave me quite a forceful speech: 'You've been of service to the club but you're still not at the right physical level, you're not ready to last ninety minutes.' It was the last straw. I had finally been a full member of the team in the last few months. I only required normal physical preparation to be at the level of my teammates. Once again, I was having to fight to prove what I could do.

It was my typical step back: fight off the difficulties to scrape full membership of the team. Wagneau Eloi, the Haitian striker, then came along; other names circulated on the list of possibilities in the football magazines. I saw them reeled off: Nicolas Goussé, who was scoring at the time, Tony Vairelles, international . . . But nothing was decided. It wasn't encouraging to hear these rumours. The group was being built and I was an extra part.

Marchand had announced to us, at the pre-season training course at Roscoff, that he wanted to recruit Christophe Le Roux, Néstor Fabbri and Jean-Louis Montero. It was a sign of Guingamp's ambition, a trigger. The club was equipping itself to survive intense times. I wanted to be a part of it. As a full member of the team.

Besides, all the guys liked me. They nicknamed me Chico, from a popular advert, due to the tuft of hair on top of my head. Bardon, who was a star and was promoted to the striker position, reassured me straightaway: 'So Chico, it's looking hot for you. Don't worry, you're our centre forward. Me, I'm more of a passer.' Kouassi added: 'Be serious and it'll happen.' Coco Michel gave me an identical speech. From the fight to stay up a team spirit was born, a kind of unfailing solidarity. This bond was almost like family, and family is sacred.

We were working like crazy together and their point of view strengthened me. Without realising it, they'd given me an enormous boost.

That didn't stop Marchand from benching me against Lyon, the French champions, on 2 August 2002. We were trailing (3–1) and the trainer threw me on for the last twenty minutes. Fortunately, my substitute experience at Le Mans had prepared me for these late entrances: I knew how to warm up, prepare myself and get out there. In the last three minutes we scored two goals, first by Bardon and then me in added time. This match launched my season. The broadcast on Canal+ boosted my comeback. I heard some of the compliments: 'Who is this guy?' Just after my goal, I took off my shirt and showed off a Nike T-shirt while the club was being sponsored by Adidas. A gesture not much appreciated by the management . . .

The coach picked me to start the following match with Ajaccio (2–0). With my first action, I opened the scoring. To this day, I still don't know how I got so high to place my header. A tremendous goal.

The good times came one after another until a new injury. I knew I had to keep proving myself to my coach, that I was constantly being questioned. At one training session I kicked the goalpost out of exasperation. An accident. I went to see Marchand: 'I don't think I can play this weekend.' 'Really, it's nothing, we'll just put ice on it.' The X-ray confirmed my prognosis: a cracked bone in my foot. One month's rest.

I went back to individual training, which I don't like. I wasn't in the mood for it. I felt picked on more than the others. Actually I came back at Troyes, at the start of November. We won there (2–0): I was never taken off the team again. What can you say about our Dream Team? When you have Flo putting in killer passes, football is never the same. He knew there was someone to receive his crosses. Besides, he wasn't the only passer. Don't forget Carnot, Hakim Saci, Bardon . . . To be centre forward with guys of this quality forces you to perform. A good striker must be able to score 20 goals per season. They were there to set up goals for me. Their altruism stunned me. At Guingamp, you played for the number 9. Our understanding developed over the course of the matches. With Marchand as well.

I appreciated him, after our rocky start . . . I didn't forget his first speech, but I interpreted it in my own way: 'Thanks for everything you've done this last year Didier, but we're looking for a real striker.' I showed him that in the end, that striker was me.

Guingamp moved to the beat of our team. This town of 9,000 inhabitants attracted 14,000 spectators. Maybe people came to see the yokels play, but at least they came. The jeers made no difference to us. A spirit of incredible camaraderie blew through the group. Not one guy spoke badly about his rival. I hadn't felt an atmosphere like it anywhere. We encouraged each other without ulterior motives. We'd had such a hard time the year before that we were benefiting from our unimaginable enthusiasm. Little clans formed according to affinities and age. The tribe of Christophe Le Roux, Stéphane Carnot, Coco Michel, the veterans, the old comrades . . . The younger players were represented by Farid Talhaoui, Steeve Joseph-Reinette, Alaeddine Yahia. My crew included Blaise Kouassi, Gérard Gnanhouan, Malouda and Jawad El Hajri, my friend. In the morning in the locker room, we told our stories. Everyone got a kick out of it. Even today, nobody can take away these memories from us. Whenever we see each other, one look is enough. It's a great feeling.

By the middle of the season we were joint second in L1 with Nice, one point behind Marseille. Massive. We were reminded of Néstor Fabbri's remarks when he arrived, tinted with his Argentinian accent: 'Hey guys, we're going to play in Europe.' We replied: 'Wait a while Néstor.' In December, this prophecy didn't seem so improbable, even if we continued to look over our shoulders.

On a personal level, I finished 2002 in third place in the ranking of strikers with eight goals, level with Anderson, just behind Nonda and Pauleta. For a first season in Ligue 1, this wasn't peanuts. My first impressions were confirmed: it was easier to score in D1 than in D2. In this division, above all, the striker plays full-out at every moment. He's on fire all the time. And then some. The changes in pace demand a better understanding of the game, a finer reading. You must be able to move from fifth gear to neutral or instead to first.

Physically, it was less intense than I thought. I just had to give the call to see the ball arrive at my feet. The guys kept on putting me in. Sometimes I thought all I had to do was push the ball into the net. I felt more easily rewarded for my efforts. But technically and tactically, that had nothing to do with it. The slightest mistake was expensive.

I realised it perfectly in January, a fatal month for our gang. Six straight defeats will lead to a very difficult winter break. It's the only time the group really got worried. Fabbri told me to move more, I replied he should measure his passes better: only what you'd expect in uncertain times. I felt, with the team, a cold wind that wintry January. I no longer found spaces. Accumulated stresses, matches and fatigue made me less sharp and so less skilful. And those eight goals had changed the perception of our opponents.

I noticed how they ran and positioned themselves to close me down . . . These developments forced me to work differently and find new solutions. Against Angoulême, in the French Cup, an old mate told me how the defenders had studied my style. I also paid attention to how others played. Pauleta, Darcheville and Nonda impressed me. Their way of creating chances in spite of close marking amazed me. I felt far inferior to them with my short professional history and lack of experience. It was beautiful to see a guy eradicate an opponent. I studied Henry and Raul and I asked myself: how do they do it sometimes? They had this capability to score at any moment, from any angle. Like Henry against Ajax or Manchester City, two matches etched in my memory. I wasn't obsessed by personal goal-scoring any more. Victories were my ultimate motivation.

We were consumed by this frame of mind and the group didn't give up mentally. We stayed united.

We knew we had to work as a team to make up for some of our players' weaknesses. That was our strength. The defeat in round three of the French Cup in Angoulême on 15 February 2003 (0–0, 3–2 on penalties) hit our morale. It was one loss too many. It caused a crisis meeting before a vital opportunity against PSG.

Paris came in the nick of time. The away match at the Parc des Princes had turned into a disaster (5–0). I had been in the stands due to my injury and I had learned this lesson. We had a score to settle. After 55 minutes of the home game, PSG rediscovered its authority (2–0) led by a magnificent Ronaldinho. He'd taken his famous shot at the end of an extraordinary slalom through our defence. One of the goals of the year. Were we going to go under? Not quite. In a giddy second half we won 3–2, with two personal goals, the last almost in the final second. It was allowed. Guingamp again became the Guingamp from the start of the season. I'd encountered the war of the warriors against Pochettino and Heinze, the Parisian defenders, guys who tried to rile me, provoke me. They needled me and I responded. I didn't want to lose against Paris, against my town.

After PSG it was fantastic. Nothing was stopping us despite

a defeat against Sedan (2–0). We played Marseille at the Vélodrome (2–0), where I scored one of our two goals. We managed a cracking tie at Sochaux (0–0), during the era of Pedretti and Frau. Guingamp was walking on water.

We beat Lens (1–0) then Monaco (3–1) at home, in the last match of the season at Roudourou, in front of 16,000 wild fans. The night was legendary – I'd never known such a rave-up. We sang song after song. The blood-alcohol level soared as the champagne went down. Everybody was a little punch-drunk. At midnight we decided to go to the hotel pool . . . Stéphane Carnot then chose to go fishing for lobsters in the giant aquarium! Others plunged in with him. An unbelievable moment of release. In the morning, the trip home. We had to face up to our wives. I was walking tall, and I came to collect my things before leaving for Lyon. The day was painful . . .

Four days later, we defied the champions, Lyon, at Gerland. We pictured them giving us a thrashing. We repeated: 'They're going to kill us.' Before this night we were shadows of ourselves, tired, ready for a hiding. This was our last match with Flo at Guingamp. Like a miracle, it was one of our greatest moments. We were the last of the club's scorers in this incredible victory (4–1). We both received a score of 8 in *L'Equipe*. This last get-together was a crowning moment. The party of parties. When Florent scored his goal, we all ran to the bench to soaring cheers. It was tremendous, a unique fellowship. Jean-Louis Montero ran past the bench imitating the noise of a cash register. He yelled to our young substitutes:

'Guys, get ready for bonuses!' Noël Le Graët, the chairman, had agreed to double them for the final act.

In the corridor, before the match, I'd run into Eric Carrière, who congratulated me and added: 'You have to come here.' Then Juninho came up to speak to me on the pitch. 'You have to come to Lyon, you'll score lots of goals and we'll still be the champions.' Wow! Coming from Juninho, the star, this touched me. Without knowing it, he had woken me up and set me free! Maybe he shouldn't have . . . Lyon's president Jean-Michel Aulas had then declared to the press: 'Tonight we saw an unstoppable player.' I'd gone out on a high note.

We left, we from Guingamp, on a last cloud of happiness, having taken three points from the champions. It was time for me to grow. I'd seen Noël Le Graët before we went to Gerland and explained that I wanted to leave the club. I only had one year left on my contract. The chairman tried everything to keep me. He even invited me to his office, a rare event: 'I am giving you everything you want so that you'll stay.' Thank you, chairman, for your involvement, but my answer was still no. 'It's not the money I want; it's Marseille and Lyon I've responded to. I want one of these big clubs.'

I didn't go on bad terms; the directors understood. But I was sad to leave such a club, such teammates. Sad to close the chapter. Guingamp offered me stability, comfort. Le Graët wanted to build a team around me. The coach's confidence was a huge thing and it factored into my decision. But I'd just turned 25 and I had to move up a level. I fancied Europe, more precisely the Champions League. Marseille and Lyon could offer me that. Not Guingamp. My personal challenge was moving on to other objectives.

On a personal level, this season had earned me my share of rewards. I'd ended the championship in third place amongst the hot shots with 17 goals, ten from the right foot, six headers and one penalty. I still needed to work on free kicks and a better command of my left foot. I'd done a lot of work by upping the sessions in front of goal, practising specific moves. I made notable progress. Nonda (26) and Pauleta (23), ahead of me, deserved their places.

L'Equipe had made me its player of the year ahead of Jérôme Rothen. All these honours were satisfying; I was enjoying this late recognition. Amongst others, I'd won the *France Soir* player of the month prize in November. Former recipients were names like Anderson, Pauleta, Ronaldinho . . . I was a minor in this company. After the end of the championship, I was even invited to the Canal+ headquarters to receive a bronze award for best African in Europe. Nonda, always ahead, collected the gold and Samuel Eto'o, then at Mallorca, the silver. To be alongside these people was an immense honour. I felt small even though Africa had started to discover me. But I still expected more. Marseille and Lyon could offer it to me.

4

MARSEILLE vs LYON: A DIFFERENT KIND OF MATCH

Worse things can happen to a footballer in his life than having to make that kind of choice. With a mere one and a half years' Ligue 1 experience behind me, I suddenly found myself being chased by the top French clubs. I struggled to understand this infatuation and sudden burst of popularity. My career was taking a sharp turn but I had to get it right and make that perfect choice, the one that would take me far; all the way . . .

Marseille and Lyon got in line, as did Paris via Francis Graille its president, the third candidate. I got a call, the conversation was warm and friendly, interesting and certainly worth considering, even if my bad memories of the capital weren't exactly pushing me in that direction. I'd been taken for a ride before. PSG wasn't at the top of my list, far from it. Anyhow, everything the coach Vahid Halilhodžiç would tell my agents would soon cool down any desire for the Parc des Princes . . .

At the Forum club, near Porte Maillot, Thierno met up with Vahid to find out what it was PSG wanted, deep down. He wanted to know more about that call from Francis Graille and the club's motivations. The Bosnian's response hit hard: 'Graille calling up players? That's my job, and when I don't call, it means I'm not interested. Didier is a good player but not a great, great striker.' End of conversation, goodbye Paris. As soon as I heard about the coach's response, I said to Thierno: 'No worries, I'll just stay Marseille or Lyon's little striker . . .' Of course there was no way I could live with that kind of treatment; I've always told my agent that one of my main requirements is to be one of the coach's priorities. I'd learned the hard way that getting on well with the coach was key to a player's progress.

Francis Graille was the president, not the coach. Paris had got into the race without playing its cards right, which was weird.

This wasn't however the case with the other two top French clubs. I already had a great experience of those cities, as at the Vélodrome and Gerland alike my end-of-match substitutions got me a standing ovation, as though the supporters were ready to welcome me with open arms. Before the end of the championship, I got a first call from Paul Le Guen, the Olympique Lyonnais coach. He told me that he was interested but that we'd have to wait a little because Sonny Anderson's future was still uncertain: was he going to leave or carry on for another season? Le Guen did say that I was up against some stiff competition with Sidney Govou and Péguy Luyindula, who was a guy he particularly liked . . . To be honest, I was actually expecting words of encouragement like: 'It may be tough but you will play.'

I wasn't all that bothered by this way of working until Olympique de Marseille came to me two days later. Alain Perrin, the Marseille coach, was much more aggressive in his approach. He assured me from the word go that I was his number one target and gave a detailed description of the part I'd play in a 4-4-2 with Pauleta at the front. I was very keen on the project and spoke to my wife, my parents and Thierno about it, but only to them. The others weren't lucid enough and most of my friends kept telling me to go to OM, speaking with their hearts when what I really needed was reason. It wasn't easy, even for me.

Because Marseille was the club I'd always dreamed of. I hadn't supported Paris, Lyon or Nantes when I was younger, but OM. Abédi Pelé, Chris Waddle, Jean-Pierre Papin, Basile Boli, I knew them all. The Le Mans training centre was actually split in half at the time of our national derby between the kings of the Canebière and PSG. It was like the Cold War. Of course, being the OM fan that I was, I kept telling my friend Frédéric Thomas: 'That's where I'm going to play.' It was Fabrizio Ravanelli's team. Thomas laughed at me. He often says to me now: 'I know what OM means to you . . .'

So the two clubs had made their first move – the battle was on. Both had the major advantage of having a place in the Champions League. That was a determining factor and the preliminary round OM had to put itself through didn't scare me off; I even found the idea exciting.

What made me lean towards following my heart were the two coaches' different approaches. I felt like Le Guen didn't want me as badly as Perrin did. Maybe it was just the way he spoke or addressed the players, but I thought: 'He's not getting in too deep because if he doesn't put me in the line-up and I complain, he'll be able to say "I told you so."' With Perrin, things were crystal clear: 'You've got your place in OM.' There was time for me to think and to talk about it still, to weigh up the pros and cons without rushing things. I couldn't hold on to my first impression, I'd just have to listen to the arguments of the two clubs and not rush into anything. I was in control.

I thought carefully about every detail. Lyon boasted some great passers like Carrière, Juninho, Dhorasoo and Govou. Jean-Michel Aulas, the president, had created the biggest French machine. At OM, the president/coach duo of Bouchet and Perrin had managed in just one year to put some order into a club that could be quite eruptive at times. That third place gleaned at the end of the season proved that much. So then?

Obviously, all the first signs pointed towards OM, which had the major added advantage that Pape Diouf, my agent, lived in the Canebière. Bouchet had wasted no time in organising a visit to the Commanderie training ground with him. I'd told Pape then that I was leaning towards Marseille, but Aulas, who was an exceptional negotiator, was hanging in there, charming Lalla and using Florent Malouda as bait. Flo wanted to join Lyon, as did his Brazilian wife, who was likely to find quite a few of her fellow countrywomen over there. To be honest, my wife would have liked to go to Lyon too . . . Aulas even sent her a gorgeous bunch of flowers, a touching gesture. He had enough experience to know that the wife is often the one who makes the final decision, so I'd found that nice and quite clever of him . . . As the negotiations went on, I went over the pros and cons, time and time again. Sure, Lyon was offering me the safety of a stable structure, the assurance of being a champion and competing in the top division every year. My eyes would open wide whenever I'd hear people talk about Lyon, this European heavyweight. My parents also preferred to see me go there; they found OM too unstable, the Vélodrome sometimes difficult with its forwards, capable of both the best and worst.

I myself tended to be less objective with regard to OM, speaking with a fan's passion. Pape had even said to me that I thrived under pressure, just like Marcel Desailly who'd almost signed with Monaco before going to OM. His career profile was flawless. The Rock's quietness wasn't a good enough match for his character; Pape could see some of Desailly in the way I approached major matches, pushing myself beyond my own limits. So OM should suit me: that was how he saw it. As time went by Marseille continued to gain the advantage. But still nothing was set.

I was meant to go and join the Ivory Coast team in Abidjan for an eliminatory match for the 2004 African Cup, and I intended to make my final decision whilst over there, in my home town. Bernard Lacombe, the Lyon president's special adviser and a former major striker, joined me to discuss the Lyon project. He left a number 11 shirt labelled with my name as a present in my hotel room, a lovely gesture. I'd liked what he said and we'd chatted, striker to striker. He'd sold OL to me brilliantly. We've actually always kept in touch; I still send him text messages to say Happy New Year. I liked the way Lyon behaved towards me and I have to take my hat off to those officials: they showed me respect. If I'd gone for Lyon, I'm sure I would have had nothing to complain about. Lacombe did everything he could to convince Thierno, even taking a taxi with him to the airport. He'd really gone for it and pulled out all the stops, but my heart belonged to Marseille and had finally spoken.

Still, nothing was definite until the contract was signed. Aulas went for yet another offensive; he had Flo called up and then Eric Carrière who was on a pre-season training placement, just to get me confused. Even as I announced my choice, the president didn't give up on getting me in, though by then it was impossible for my decision to be reversed. They couldn't have done a better job of selling OL to me and I can really see why the club is doing so well.

I felt bad towards Bernard Lacombe. When he called me, I think Aulas was there too. I warned: 'I picked Marseille.' 'Are you sure?' 'Yes.' A few days later, OL was still trying. I would actually have earned a lot more with Lyon, an extra 25,000 or 30,000 euros per month, but it wasn't about the money, and Marseille was also making me quite comfortable financially, no point in denying it. It was a huge amount for me; I felt like I was gleaning the fruit of my work, of those years of struggle. I hadn't been lucky enough to get an early start and I could of course have just wanted to fill up my bank account, but I was focused on the team; my feelings more important than anything else. You have to know what your priorities are.

When I got back from South Africa where I was playing an eliminatory African Cup of Nations match, I went and signed my contract. Guingamp, having bought me for 150,000 euros, was now getting 6 million; the club certainly did well out of it . . . When I saw the Marseille shirt for the first time with my name and the number 11 on it, it did something major to me. It was Chris Waddle's, Eric Cantona's. I was hoping for that number, but it was Cyril Chapuis's already. I didn't want to cause trouble in the team and force him to hand it over, but Perrin assured me that he was leaving anyway. I felt a little beholden to him. I was happy, I'd signed with the club I wanted and I'd got my lucky number 11 back. The adventure was about to begin.

First, I went to the Dominican Republic for twelve days. It was the first time I was going on holiday with my whole little family . . . wonderful times. I met a PSG supporter who became a great friend. At the time, people were talking about me at OM and Lyon but he wanted me in Paris. He insisted on taking a picture of me wearing a PSG shirt. Oh no, not that

. . . During this break, I'd also decided to work out to come back fit. I was so worried about being out of shape when I came in that I'd prepared a regular jogging schedule. I'd never done any solo preparation before; was this keeping fit going to yield results?

I came back to the Commanderie, our training place, in the hot and sunny South of France. I was suffering in the physical training sessions, as we were in the middle of a heat wave and Roger Propos, the fitness coach, was really manhandling us. I thought the wristwatch that measured my pulse was going to explode as my heart rate went up to 200, 215 beats, emitting a continuous beep which indicated I was going into overdrive. I was lost right from the first running session. Johnny Ecker, the defender, turned around and said to the others: 'Look guys, Didier's fallen behind, let's wait for him.' He brought me to the front and everyone followed me. At my own pace . . . That's when I thought: 'That guy really is amazing. This is my club, I made the right choice.' The staff, the physios were winding me up. 'Look, the Guingamp guy's struggling!' No doubt about it: I was at Marseille. My dream club.

5

LOVE STORY

This beautiful story began in Brittany during the typical pre-season training trip, a milestone in my career with Marseille. I was sharing a room with Fabio Celestini, the Swiss player, in our hotel. He briefed me on everything, notably on Alain Perrin whom he'd known since his stint with Troyes. 'This is how he's going to react, but don't mind him, that's what he's like. Don't go changing, keep doing your thing.' These simple little words were of great help in that they made tackling the club and its trainer much easier. Celestini shortened my adjustment period and eased some of my uncertainties, even though the first matches would lead to a few misunderstandings with the public . . .

Just like some astonishing omen we started the champion-ship at Guingamp (1–0). I'd hardly had the time to get over my departure from the coasts of Armorica and I didn't manage to score against my former teammates. I wasn't very good but I morphed into a passer for Ibrahim Bakayoko, my fellow countryman, towards the end of the game. It didn't take the Vélodrome long to come up with a nickname for me: 'Drogbayoko'. I was Drogba and Bakayoko rolled into one, which basically meant that I was missing too many chances! Great start after just three weeks on the job . . . People grumbled, criticised and my sister Nadia, who came to watch a game at the Vélodrome, overheard some comments in the stands. She couldn't believe what she was hearing. 'Just what is this club? They're as rough as they are in Africa,' she told me before telling me what my nickname was. 'That's how they perceive me, but I'm going to show them,' I said to her, feeling re-energised.

I was motivated by the will to conquer. In Lens (lost 2–1), on the third day, I scored with my first touch. A header into the corner. In the same swoop, miming a flying plane, I skidded a few metres towards the corner on my knees and raised my arms. My son picked up this move and would later love doing that same skid at home, on the tiled floor. This little glimpse filled me with delight; I felt like he knew that was my first-ever goal for OM. The remainder of our evening in Lens was far less fruitful: I'd had three chances and Itandje, the Lens goalkeeper, had worked miracles.

My header made no difference so I had to take stock. I

started working twice as hard in front of goal. Nothing unusual, but some sessions with Albert Emon, who was a member of staff. All of Jean-Pierre Papin's work at the end of his years with Marseille was still fresh in my mind. I had to go through those learning stages to get a chance to grow.

Thankfully, a week after the Lens trip, something finally happened when we played against Sochaux (2–0). A dream move for my first goal at the Vélodrome. I'd shifted Johnny Ecker with a back-heel, my speciality, on the left. Then I picked up his cross outside the penalty area and volleyed a shot, skidding slightly. I could bust my plane move . . . The papers turned the picture of my celebration into a metaphor: 'Drogba takes off'. We were becoming championship leaders in an amazing atmosphere. I was already being compared to Papin and his famous 'Papinades', to Josip Skoblar, a former local star . . .

Things move very fast at OM . . . sometimes too fast. At least I was done with that slightly annoying nickname but still, the praise couldn't disguise reality. I was a long way from being as big as those guys; they represented role models to aspire to. I was just starting out on the Canebière, getting a first taste of the exhilaration yet to come. I was happy here; getting to the Commanderie in the morning was pure joy. Crossing over to the training pitch and seeing those mountains in the distance, enclosing us as you'd embrace a child, made me happy. What more was there to ask for? The warmth of the people gave me fulfilment, the results followed suit, and we'd got into the Champions League, the real deal, via Austria

Vienna in the qualifiers (1–0, 0–0). We were level with Lyon in this battle between top Europeans.

I felt like I was living the dream of my Le Mans friends, those who'd shared my love for OM watching Paris–Marseille games at the centre. I immersed myself completely and my adjustment period turned out pretty short in the end. The end of this trouble-free first act came against Le Mans (5–0) at the Vélodrome on the sixth day: we were leading in Ligue 1, two points ahead of Monaco and seven of Lyon.

That evening, a tackle by Capron had forced me out at half-time. Never mind. Mido, the Egyptian, had scored two goals and I one, but the ogre that is Real Madrid was still to come at Santiago Bernabéu.

Quite unexpectedly, something went wrong there at half-time. Perrin had already had a real go at us after our first-leg victory in Vienna (1–0), which didn't really surprise me as Celestini had warned me about that: Perrin wanted to push us to our fullest potential and he hadn't appreciated the number of missed chances in Austria one bit. He had another go at us in Madrid; it was worse that time around. Marlet had been taken out before the end of the first half, which wasn't something that happened often and was embarrassing for him. Then the coach was really hard on Habib Beye during the break, raising his tone a notch, two even . . . That scene had an impact on the group who stood there without reacting. I'll come back to our European journey in the next chapter.

Feeling fragile after this major incident, we moved on to Nantes (1–0) five days later. Perrin had come across an interview with our goalkeeper Vedran Runje in *France Football* where Vedran was saying that perhaps we hadn't used the right strategy in Spain. OM went ballistic. Perrin tore him to pieces, held a grudge against him, which loosened the ties inside the team. We'd reached a phase of acute conflict and weren't speaking to the coach. It felt weird. Perrin no longer managed the training sessions and let Albert Emon take the lead. He was still the boss, indirectly, but the tension was rising fast. The week before we took on Nice, in the wake of our defeat at Nantes, the coach was no longer around. Seeing the coach abandoning us like that got to me.

The atmosphere surrounding the pre-match briefing was even more bizarre, almost surreal. The staff and players stood on one side and Perrin, who'd stopped directing us and speaking to us, on the other. He did however talk to us on the eve of the match: 'OK, so let me know when you're ready and put the team together for tomorrow. It's on you guys.' I'd never come across a situation like that before. We spent most of the evening and night talking in the hotel corridor. Was this the joke it appeared to be? Runje felt guilty, he needed to be comforted and calmed down. 'If I am the problem, then let him fire me,' he said. 'I don't care, but the team shouldn't have to suffer for it. I didn't mean any harm when I talked about that.'

This was a tricky situation to handle. All of us together decided that we wouldn't pick the team. No way, it wasn't our job. 'It isn't up to us to do that. He's the coach, let him do it, he's the one who has to pick the side, that's what he's being paid for!' When he asked us to give him our eleven, we didn't answer, so he had to give in. He gave us his list and the mood was chilly as we headed to the Vélodrome. The players were saying, 'He's letting us down; we've got to find our own way. We're a family, let's all stick together. We're going to show him what we can do, that we're real men.'

At half-time, we got back to the dressing room trailing 1–0; the coach still wasn't saying a word. Albert Emon intervened, briefly. That's when I got up and spoke out, so strong was my frustration. I blew a fuse. 'Guys, let's get moving, we can't lose by just one goal. They could be two ahead if they hadn't missed a sitter. We need to do everything we can to wake up the fans and win them over. That'll do the trick.' We got up, talked amongst ourselves; everyone chipped in. 'If you do this, I'll do that; got to push on, not lose so many one-on-ones . . .' I managed a brace in the second half, one of which was a goal during injury time. Some major achievement in a mood that swung around to our advantage by the time the final whistle blew. That night positioned me as a leader. I wasn't claiming anything, it just happened naturally; times like this brought some people out of themselves, allowed them to emerge.

In the same stride as this victory which we'd torn from our opponents as though with forceps, Perrin explained to us that his self-management method had been successful in the past, at Troyes. It was a means of making us take ownership, creating a commando spirit. Whatever, that wasn't what this team needed.

So I felt more and more involved, and was gaining a certain

degree of importance. After losing in the Champions League in Porto (1–0), in November, I'd called a meeting and opened up to the team, which went straight to the heart of some. My words were probably a little unpolished, poorly chosen, but in hindsight, the guys got it anyway. I needed to let it out because I couldn't stand it any longer, the situation was unbearable. We'd fall apart at major events. Shooting off my mouth like that was a chancy thing to do. When you're on your own, things don't always work out, but I got some support. Suddenly it wasn't just one player mumbling to himself but two or three, then eventually the whole group. We had to redouble our efforts or we'd miss something big. I couldn't just leave the team the way it was, like: 'Keep to yourself, play a match, go home.'

Not to mention that there'd been a managerial blunder with the announcement of Fabien Barthez's arrival. Fabien was showing up as number 1 in October, but for administrative reasons he couldn't play till January. Seeing as Cédric Carrasso was injured, Runje found himself in a terrible situation. Even though we had stayed together, we hadn't had the strength of character to weather that moment in the season, which is something I'm sorry about as far as he's concerned. I should've reacted more boldly. That guy was well liked by everyone, he was a leader, he was charismatic, he was one of the greats and he was tough. Under those conditions, it was unsurprising that we'd get a slap in the face in Strasbourg (4–1). Runje was upset, having just heard the news that Barthez was due to sign within the next few days.

The fact that Fabien didn't speak much didn't make it any easier on Runje. Things were really tense with the coach and since we weren't getting the results . . . We'd lost important matches against Lyon (4–1), and Monaco at home (2–1) despite leading 1–0. The vibe between the management and the coach was off and the Christmas break had done little to alleviate tensions. Around mid-January, following a defeat at Auxerre (2–0) with us in sixth position and one or two matches in hand over our nearest rivals, Perrin was given his marching orders. Really, not all was lost, even though we were stuck on a very poor series of 10 defeats in 16 matches, five of them at the Vélodrome, since that famous Strasbourg episode . . .

Our loss to Auxerre in Burgundy had been catastrophic. A weird match, a team without heart; I'd never felt that way before. We didn't stick together and we were all guilty.

Still, letting Perrin go? I was pretty shocked that no one had even asked me what I thought about this eviction. The decision was taken by the management. Despite the occasional tensions and him being hard on us, Perrin was a man I genuinely appreciated. You could slip him a few ideas, influence him positively. He did rub me the wrong way more than once, though: 'Didier, didn't you feel like winning tonight?' 'What do you mean, I was the one providing all my own chances, so what makes you think that?' I'd experienced this kind of relationship before, with Guy Lacombe, but not everyone can handle such a strong personality. Their only demand is to bring out an individual's maximum potential, but there are other ways of dealing with players: you have to be aware of their psychological state of mind. You can't address everyone in the same manner or you're bound to lose some men along the way. A harsh comment – 'you're crap' – can elicit a reaction at either end of the spectrum; some people will bow down, others jump up. This management style didn't bother me on a personal level; it forces you to be good just to make sure your coach has nothing left to have a go at you about.

I actually even felt like dedicating my two goals to Alain Perrin after we beat Lens (3–2) after the Auxerre debacle. I waited a little before calling him, feeling a little shy . . . We were all responsible for that situation. In the end I just told him I was sorry. Even though it really affected him, Perrin handled having to leave with a great deal of detachment. He had a hard time getting over it. But he's a good man, he bounced back and has proved that he's one of the best French coaches around.

Taking over from him, José Anigo came in with a different style and with a major advantage: when you come into a team with low morale, people see you as their saviour, as someone who's going to bring back their motivation. There's a renewal of courage and eagerness. His words were in huge contrast with Perrin's: 'I'm not going to have a go at you just because you miss a pass.' There was laughter at the table, people felt better. Guys were saying to each other: 'This guy's cool, he's good. Makes a change.'

We were shifting from high tension to a gentler way of handling human relationships and a kind of friendship grew between us. We fought for José, we'd knacker ourselves out for José. This dynamic came into force, and we came out of ourselves. Guys who were already excellent, like Abdoulaye Méïté and Habib Beye, surpassed themselves. Perrin's departure freed some, relieved others and the group got stronger. Bringing in Laurent Batlles during the winter transfer period was providing new solutions in our passing game and helping Camel Meriem as a result.

I was feeling strong, seeing all those people gravitating around a single project. At first, this bond was something I had to go looking for, but then the guys got my game; they saw I was willing to sacrifice my own interests for the team. There was respect between us: that's what pleased me the most.

I was really close to Steve Marlet and Habib Beye. As a leader, it was my duty to be close to everyone, to be receptive. I like this kind of commitment. I wasn't even the captain; that duty was assigned first to Celestini then Brahim Hemdani. I occasionally got the armband when Hemdani was out, but my role went beyond this rigid framework.

I was in charge of warm-ups, having taken over from Brahim and Roger Propos, the fitness coach. It happened naturally, without any imposition on my part: I just had a chat with Roger. We were trying to change our method, the way we worked; I'd earned this respect on the pitch by always giving it my all. I didn't carry any particular tactical weight within the team; I'd ended up alone up front because Mido wasn't living up to expectations. The Egyptian had had a hard time finding his feet and Steve Marlet seemed a little more detached. He was hanging around me, but I'd never asked him to; those choices belonged to the coaches.

We worked well together and my behaviour impressed the fans. I'd hear of stuff like Drogbamania, Didyeah, Drogbut, Drogbadaboum . . . At one point, my family decided to go and buy shirts with my name on from the OM shop and there were none left. I felt proud and I couldn't disappoint. Philippe Christanval once told me: 'Let's be honest with ourselves, we're not imagining things here. You're the one holding the team together now. When you're good, the team works well; when you score, we win.' Without knowing it, he'd put even more responsibilities on me. I took his words as a token of his absolute trust in me.

My teammates were doing a lot for me and with this bountiful mood I was organising dinners, little parties. One morning I'd ended up in a complete state, half asleep with my face on the ground right in front of the house. My wife wasn't too impressed to see me coming home so tired and with the imprint of gravel on my face . . .

I actually never left the Commanderie early, which got me scolded. 'What is it you're doing there, why are you always home so late?' I'd found my little piece of heaven. I was happy.

My role was to bring people together. When one of the guys had problems, we'd talk about them; some drew on my strength at the time to sort them out. I'd listen to the physio, to the woman who did the laundry, to the cleaning lady. A club is a family; you have to give these people back the love they give you. We had an hour and a half a week to give them magical moments and there was no getting it wrong. There comes a point where all you need is to know when to listen. It's in my nature. The hard times we'd been through had created a strong comradeship.

Still, I never felt like OM's superstar: that would inevitably have caused problems. There was no way I was setting myself apart from the team. My experience with lower-profile clubs did a lot to help me in my approach.

I'd met some genuine stars like Coco Michel, Cédric Bardon, Christophe Le Roux, Néstor Fabbri, Blaise Kouassi . . . They'd all stayed humble. I couldn't change; without any false modesty, without my teammates I was nothing and I definitely didn't see myself as heaven-sent.

Yes, of course I won quite a lot of awards but there was only one thing I really wanted: to win a trophy with OM. This final goal took away any kind of individualistic spirit. Yet all I was getting were individual rewards, which I found weird and paradoxical.

Our European journey had used up some of our championship energy, hence our average season. We didn't have the strength to chase up two competitions at the same time: we realized this and focused our energy on the UEFA Cup. But I have fond memories of my last game with OM at the Vélodrome. My friends from Guingamp were playing to survive in Ligue 1. They needed to make their mark and we beat them (2–1). It was painful; I went back on the pitch to comfort my mates. Tears were rolling down Yahia's cheeks and I gave him a hug. I'd felt relegation fever on my last day with

Guingamp and I understood their bitter disappointment . . .
There was nothing I could do about it. I'd earned the player
of the month title in May, the last of the season, beating
Ludovic Giuly to it. Little did I know that this was to be my
last appearance wearing a French shirt. That year had established me.

Who would have thought that someone who one year
before was just a Guingamp substitute would win the award
for player of the year from his peers? Certainly not me. Times
like these are part of the reason to be in this job. I immediately
thought about my coaches, Loncar, Westerloppe, Pascalou,
Lacombe, Marchand, and Perrin who'd drawn me to
Marseille. They had all played a part, to a greater or lesser
extent, in my success. And of course how could I forget my
teammates? I was on cloud nine; I was ahead of Ludovic Giuly,
who'd had an extraordinary season. To tell the truth, I'd voted
for him and I wouldn't have been surprised if he'd won.

That night, TV viewers had given me the prize for finest
goal of the season in Montpellier, a volley after a rebound. I'd
enjoyed the shot myself: I'd hit a screamer after a centre from
the left.

I couldn't attend this ceremony because José Anigo didn't
want us to disperse before the UEFA Cup second-leg semi-
final against Newcastle. Behind all those awards, the greatest
one of all was still to be claimed: the European trophy.

6

EUROPEAN MADNESS

I was dreaming of discovering the Champions League. Once we'd passed the Vienna hurdle in the qualifiers, I'd waited like a child to see who'd be drawn in our group. Who was it going to be? Knowing that we were bound to end up with top-flight opponents, we were keen to find out who they were. We got Porto, Partizan Belgrade and most importantly, Real Madrid.

First European match, first trip to the Spanish capital. I could hardly have hoped for a finer baptism. It was awe-inspiring. During the tactical session the day before, I'd felt such deep emotions on that turf. Santiago Bernabéu. A cathedral. When I heard the first notes of the Champions League anthem fly into the air, memories came flooding back.

Powerful images: me and my friends, almost teenagers, having a pizza or some tea whilst watching Raul or Mijatoviç in European matches. When we got in line, I said to Abdou Méïté: 'This is it mate, we've made it!' He replied in the same excited tone, the anthem in the background adding to the solemnity of the moment. On top of it all, it was the era of star players, Zidane, Beckham, Raul, Ronaldo, Roberto Carlos, Figo and the gang. Oddly enough, I didn't feel afraid of them, I felt serene, certain that our team had what it took to achieve a thing or two over there. We could even hear our fans, we felt strong, almost at home. However, my first goal failed to unsettle them and we lost (4–2), feeling it had been a close shave . . .

Never mind, it just meant we needed to focus on Partizan Belgrade, an opponent more within our range. The first leg at the Vélodrome is still a moment of pure magic for me, coming right after a double against Nice. I'd gone out to a club on the Saturday night and a fan had come up to me: 'What the hell are you doing here? You'd better score some goals.' I wasn't in the mood for that: 'How is it any of your business what I'm doing here? Of course I'm going to score!' I said this like I was making a promise. I had no idea I was going to achieve the first hat-trick of my career. The first half had been tricky, the second superb with three goals: one with a little heel kick, another with my shoulder and the last one with the left, all in the space of twenty-three minutes!

That was our Champions League victory and the beginning of Drogbamania. The papers praised me all the more when I added yet another goal at home against Bastia the following weekend (3–1)! Six in one week, with Europe at the core of those seven days. As soon as our Partizan match finished, my voicemail filled up in a flash, with more than seventy messages. Returning friends' calls was impossible. At that point, the names on people's lips were Jean-Pierre Papin, Franck Sauzée and Josip Skoblar, who also scored a few hat-tricks for OM on the European scene. I was touched by these comparisons, even though my memories of international strikers were limited to Papin, Rudi Völler, Sonny Anderson, Alen Bokšiç, and less so Skoblar, who was older. In the same sweep, I was winning the spot of best striker in the Champions League, which was almost unheard of for a 25-year-old player without much of a track record. I had to pinch myself to believe it.

Porto would soon bring us back down to earth, back to our lack of experience, though years later José Mourinho's exceptional training programme made up for the disappointment I felt at the time. We lost both matches against Porto and that strengthened the control of the likes of Deco, Derlei, Maniche and Costinha. Later on, the Portuguese would dish out other lessons, to Lyon for instance, before earning the supreme title against Monaco (3–0). They'd brought down all the stars of French football in their quest for the Grail. At any rate, those two setbacks had scuppered our prospects of reaching the Champions League knockout rounds. What a disappointment. In the second leg, we lost 1–0 in the Estádio do Dragão and I'd even hit the bar with a free kick right on the whistle. Could this lift our hopes? Not really.

We still had to make sure we didn't mess up against Partizan, a hurdle we could actually handle. We managed a 1–1 draw with Jérémy Gavanon in goal, Runje dropping to the bench. Tough.

We were tumbling into the UEFA Cup without any certainties. We no longer even considered it a target, so powerful was our disappointment after we were eliminated. Dnepropetrovsk as our opponent in the third round didn't sound like one of Europe's greatest, more like an obligation.

We won the first leg at the Vélodrome in a doomsday mood (1–0), with hardly a soul in the stadium. It felt like a mock game, the dressing room dead despite the victory. Even the goal I scored meant nothing: I'd scored a penalty but as I shot, my supporting leg had gone from under me and the ball had hit my left foot before going in!

At the end of the match, OM's hundredth in a European Cup, quite the event, we felt like we weren't up to scratch and that we hadn't taken this meeting seriously enough. The trainers and Christophe Bouchet, the president, slammed us. He lost it with us. With a tone that required no explanation and would tolerate no answer, he said: 'The UEFA Cup is an objective for this club! You need to show this tournament some respect and you better get qualified out there.' His words made us aware of just how important this competition was. We didn't have the right to shame it. This turned out to be the founding gesture of our journey. We went to Ukraine wanting to win something: we did everything we could to qualify. I would actually never have set foot there without this sporting goal . . .

It was cold, the pitch felt greasy and José Anigo had sent me to rest on the bench. I'd only gone on for about twenty minutes and we'd made it out of the trap (0–0). This is when we started on our way. Mathieu Flamini had just joined the team, he was just a boy and he wanted to mingle. He liked me. On the flight back, Hemdani and I were discussing bonuses and Mathieu joined our conversation. He started by saying: 'I'm happy to be here with you guys.' He was discovering the professional world. We did the best we could to make him feel at ease, to get him into the swing of things. He was hungry for knowledge and wanted to blend in with more senior players, waiting in the shadows.

We were already talking about our next opponents in the fourth round. Most of us were hoping for Liverpool, and we ended up drawing the Reds! Playing at Anfield was beautiful but hard. I found myself up front, with Marlet for support, in a face-off with Henchoz and Hyypiä, one of the finest pairings in Europe. This was a genuine battle. Right from the start I felt this would be my match. I thought: 'I'm going to score, I'll make the difference.' They scored against us in the second half then I matched it fifteen minutes from the end off a cross from Meriem.

I broke the offside trap, took out Finnan, and scored (1–1). This equaliser gave me strength. That night, I proved to myself that I was capable of imposing myself against heavyweight, top-level defenders. In my own way, I was making my mark on the short history of French football. You had to scroll back 27 years to find the last (and only) time a French goal had been scored against Liverpool. Dominique Bathenay had done it with Saint-Etienne during a match they lost against the wonderful team that included Kevin Keegan (3–1). Those were the days of the big Greens and the legendary shirt I'd kept as a relic since my youth, courtesy of Michel Goba, my uncle.

The players had sung to me in the dressing room because that 11 March was also the day of my 26th birthday. This 'happy birthday' had annoyed Gérard Houllier, the Reds' coach, who judged this loudness to be inappropriate, even though it had nothing to do with showing off or making fun of the English.

That draw made the second leg, at the Vélodrome, even more uncertain, with Heskey opening the scoring after fifteen minutes. They manhandled us for thirty minutes, the back half slaving away like ants, trying to get a touch of the ball. Then we were given a penalty after a foul by Bišćan on Marlet at the edge of the penalty area, which got the defender sent off. I hit it full-strength under the bar. One hour into the game, my friend Méïté knocked in a header past Dudek (2–1). By the last ten minutes, there was no way back for Liverpool; we'd made it into the quarter-finals.

The draw brought us Inter Milan. On the day of the first leg, at home, I had a dodgy knee and wasn't feeling on top of my game. The pain persisted, and in the afternoon I rang the bursar, Lionel Bourroux, to confess that I probably wouldn't be able to play. He took me to see Lionel Castellonese, the club's osteopath, some 40 km away. He fixed me up. I hadn't had a chance to rest before coming up against Inter's star players. No siesta; stress more like. Playing against Cannavaro, Cordoba, Vieri, I was expecting the worst. Inter had sent in the big guys and this was an UEFA Cup quarter-final! Still, I managed to score right at the start of the second half. I climbed up the fence to dedicate this goal to my wife as it was her birthday. A special day. Problem: the referee, who wasn't a fan of such public displays of affection, gave a yellow card, meaning I was suspended for the second leg. My disappointment lasted five minutes, about as long as it takes to get over a broken toy. It was intense but brief.

After that, I did my utmost to score. I wanted to finish them off but I couldn't. It wasn't happening. I was devastated, even though we should have got a penalty after a foul on Meriem in the box.

In a way, I felt I'd let my mates down, but they came up to me and said: 'Didier, we'll win this for you.' Wow! Hearing them speak those words gave me goose bumps. Our European history was being born. We were fighting for one another. Meriem's game reached a very high level. He became the team detonator, our little technical advantage. You could also sense a willingness to live out a team adventure. Our ties with the public were getting stronger. I had one obsession that wouldn't leave me alone: we couldn't mess up against Milan. Without me there.

I watched the second leg from the stands, wearing a suit, tense as a bowstring. When Meriem delivered a goal after showing his pace (1–0), taking advantage of a dummy run by Steve Marlet, I erupted. A goal fifteen minutes before the end, a goal that opened the way to fulfilling our dreams. No doubt about it. OM got its semi-final and I could join my mates on the pitch and give Meriem a hug. The boys had done it, had given me a wonderful present. San Siro filled with the noise of 5,000 hysterical fans. They'd stuck around, applauding and cheering for long minutes of absolute ecstasy. We heard that the people of Marseille had gathered around the Old Port, that the city had opened its shutters and quite simply refused to go to sleep.

I felt relieved that the team had managed to qualify without me. The semi-final against Newcastle was drawing nearer, which meant another trip to the North of England for our first meeting in St James's Park, another football cathedral. Before us stood Alan Shearer, the legend. An exceptional player through his longevity and sense of purpose. Before our duel, I'd mentioned his tendency to elbow people and Shearer had said: 'I've always used my elbows, I can't see the problem as long as I'm not hurting anyone.' He was 33 and this impressed me, made him seem eternal.

That evening in England (0–0) left me with one particular memory: I'd run around all over the place, I'd hit Given's post with a volley then seen another ball stopped by a defender on the line. I felt disappointed, like I hadn't got enough offensive support. Everyone was pleased with the result, but I felt frustrated.

Some teammates didn't get my reaction but I felt over-whelmed with emotion and it was difficult to shake it off. The number of matches was beginning to take its toll on my body. The second leg was something special. After Monaco's achievement in the Champions League, everyone was expecting us to do well in the UEFA Cup. This match could open the door to the final; bring back memories of a glorious past. The city was displaying an unbelievable passion.

Unfortunately I suffered a groin strain, which had forced me to train on my own on the eve of the game. I'd worked with Jean-Philippe Durand, Laurent Spinosi and Jérémy Gavanon, the second goalie. My idea was to concentrate on quick runs, rehearsing what might happen during the match: little touches, tricks in the goal mouth, two-metre accelerations, nothing too complicated. On D-Day, I felt ready to lead the club to the final. It was my job. I got the fact that a whole nation expected great things from us, so I'd put a huge amount of pressure on myself. I kept telling myself: 'Get us qualified! Do everything to get there.'

My prayers were heard. I scored the kind of goal I'd always dreamed of. I went off on a run from a pass by Meriem, I turned Hughes inside out with a back-heel and struck with my left foot. I'd practised this sequence whilst training at Le Mans. What a long journey it had been from Le Mans to Newcastle . . . I drove in the second goal from a Lolo Batlles free kick, thanks to a move by Marlet and Méïté who'd pulled their markers away from me. We were in the final. The final!

The atmosphere that night was amazing. During warm-up, the stadium was as bubbly as if we'd just won. In times like these the mood is so powerful that it's hard to stay focused.

The risk is to get carried away and give everything before the actual clash, running out of steam just as things get started. I felt so good that I tried stuff I never usually dare to do otherwise. The context helped me push beyond my own boundaries, to outdo myself.

I felt immense relief; I'd had a difficult month because of my general tiredness. It had got me down. People got me back on track; I stopped getting unnecessarily wound up. Thank God I had loyal teammates without whom none of this would have been possible. No one cheated or got sneaky. In José Anigo I also had a coach who knew how to manage me; he had passion and he wore it on his sleeve, sometimes he overreacted but he loved his team. You have to respond to that. We were living out a beautiful adventure and he was influential in it. He gave me a certain degree of responsibility. He'd never push me when I wasn't feeling on top of my game. 'Don't worry. I know you'll get it in. I trust you; you'll be great next time.' Whenever I felt tired, I'd train alone. Especially towards the end of the season. I wasn't used to having to cope with such a hellish pace. Those two goals against Newcastle and this place in the final also came as a reward for Anigo's self-belief; the European Cup was all we were living for, much like our fans were.

Our mistakes and the losses to Lyon and Monaco had long extinguished our meagre hopes for the league title. Our fans understood that we didn't have the strength to fight on two fronts. We were betting on Europe, unwittingly doubling our investment in the Continental nights. The public enjoyed the show so much that they tended to forgive us; our win over

Newcastle was the most obvious proof. The stadium seemed in a torrent of passion. Unfortunately for me, ten days before the final we went to Monaco. The Champions League finalists against the UEFA Cup finalists. Quite the line-up. That was one of my low times: I was dragging my feet a bit and having a hard time keeping it up going from game to game.

So José had asked me how I felt about playing that day and had put me on the bench. I don't really like warming up during the match, and José brought me on in the second half. In contesting a ball in the air, I jumped for a header at the same time as Julien Rodriguez came in to stop me jumping or maybe to do some damage. He kneed me in the hip and I fell, seeing stars. I felt numb; perhaps Rodriguez had hit a nerve. All the same, I pushed myself straight into the final ten days later. I just couldn't miss it. That was stupid.

I went to the Princess Grace Hospital in the Principality. I stayed there but nothing showed up on the X-ray. The bus waited for me for an hour and a half.

I felt like a cripple in Gothenburg, where we faced Valencia in the final act of the UEFA competition. I felt like I was being electrocuted each time I tried to run or strike. I just couldn't play effectively; that final was a nightmare. I couldn't help my teammates the way I wanted to, I could only give 40 or 50 per cent against the Spanish champions. Aimar, Mista, Ayala were all there . . . We dominated the first fifteen, twenty minutes; they didn't manage to bring out their style. Then the match evened out until Valencia created a chance and Barthez came out with his foot a bit too high. The famous Italian referee

Gianluigi Collina blew the whistle and sent off our goalie on the basis that he'd prevented a certain goal.

This decision put paid to our chances. In fact, right from my first ball, those Valencia guys knew how to handle me: Ayala had elbowed me in the neck to take me out. This is a South American and generally Latin speciality. I had a hard time getting up.

Ten minutes in, the mission became impossible. We gave away a second goal: the writing was on the wall. I'd often heard people talk about Mr Collina as the best referee in the world: I knew some in the French championship who were much better, but far less on view in the media. He was the star of the match. But the stars should have been the players of the two teams. His decision to send off Barthez ruined the final. When Collina gave him the red card at the end of the first half, I went to see him and said: 'Look at the clock, can't you see how much time there is left?' He answered that he had to follow the rules.

But sometimes you need to adapt to the situation and circumstances of the game. In fact, during Euro 2004, when David James, the English goalie, took out Henry, all he got was a yellow card. At least he got the chance to defend his goal; Fabien didn't.

After that, everything went really fast. Jérémy Gavanon came on and Camel Meriem left. I wouldn't have made the same decision, which is something I brought up with José later on. But things move so quickly in times like these . . .

Valencia was the only team in the European Cup (with the exception of the third qualifying round against Vienna) I'd failed to score against. I'd always found an opening before, whether with Real (1), Partizan (3), Porto (1), Dniepr (1), Liverpool (2), Inter (1) or Newcastle (2), but not with the Spaniards.

This came as a huge disappointment, even if with 11 goals I'd ended up as the best striker in the European tournaments. We were so close to the title. I'd rather be eliminated in the semi-final than beaten in the final. Those kinds of slaps stay with you for ever. I could already picture myself showing off the trophy at the Vélodrome, parading through the city's streets . . . I sometimes think about that, even years later, and tell myself that if I'd been 100 per cent, this game could have gone differently. I did get a few chances but I couldn't make a difference, couldn't find space, couldn't fight on equal terms.

I wanted to make it to the end so badly that this abrupt halt crushed me. Marseille had made me emotional. Compared with some great strikers we'd come up against, I'd done some good things. When I got to the Canebière, I was told it would be tough. I knew it and I did everything I could to make things easier for myself. I tried to listen to those who talked to me and gave me advice. Tried not to let it get to me. I could have ended up just like some players who crashed and burned within two or three months with OM and who were never heard of again. Those who lasted were those who kept their feet on the ground and didn't get put off. You can't come to OM thinking: I'm going to shine. It's way too hard. You have to be proud to be wearing that shirt, because titles can be won there. I'd missed my chance. Sure, I'd get another; at least that was what I thought back then. I never thought that door would be slammed right in my face.

7

DECLARING MY LOVE

How can I explain this passion which borders on insanity? Words sometimes fail me. The virus has spread through my blood, the blood of a long-time fan. I loved this club even before I joined it; I fell head over heels for it. One season was all it took for it to steal my heart. That year packed in the emotions of ten.

It all started at the Vélodrome Stadium, in that seething volcano. I'd come with Daniel Cousin, my friend from Le Mans, to see Marseille play Lyon, and it came as a shock to the system. I fell under the spell of this unreal atmosphere and spent just as long watching the two Kops chanting at one another as following the actual game. I was about to discover this stadium with an OM shirt on my back.

Strangely enough, it took me a while to lose my inhibitions about this stadium; at first I could hardly stand it for more than an hour. After that I felt like I was choking, couldn't feel my legs, could hardly breathe; it was the excitement, this feeling that I was living a unique moment, and the stress was making me legless. I could hear that anthem, Van Halen's 'Jump', blaring as I walked down the corridor; I could see the stand on my left, like a wall of fans. Such an amazing feeling as I left the dressing room, hearing this deafening noise, seeing those huge crowd displays.

Playing against Auxerre (1–0), when I was just starting out, I had goose bumps. As the months went by I began to feel completely at one with the supporters. I'd hear them sing this song in my honour ('Didier Drogbalalalalala'), which made me feel weightless, as though I was really elsewhere. It was a fusion thing; we all loved the same club, they loved it from the stands and I from the pitch. When playing, I was really a fan dressed for the job. I'd become a part of this madness. When Florent Malouda showed up to watch me play against Inter for the UEFA Cup, he was blown away. 'Didier, I want to come as well.' He'd got it too. I've never felt this kind of symbiosis with any other city. It was huge. The stadium felt like it was exploding every time I scored and it had become a kind of game between us. We'd egg each other on; I'd get the fans going and they gave as good as they got. They gave me their all. I can still picture myself facing this stand and this delirious crowd chanting my name, standing there bare-chested, swinging my shirt above my head with these thousands of people responding in their own way, with words and gestures. How could you begin to withstand such displays of fervour? Those were times when I no longer felt like a footballer but rather like a plane, ready to fly over the pitch.

The Vélodrome welcomed me with a giant picture of myself and a phrase like an invocation: 'Drogba, score for us.' I was one of them, they were proud that I'd picked OM. I was there to give them joy; they came to the stadium to feel ecstasy, to get their fill. It was a festival. I resorted to the crowd to get myself going again. I'd give them goals, they gave me their warmth in return. I've always loved interacting with the crowds, getting a reaction out of them. It's the showman in me.

Still, sometimes these shows of love would stretch my boundaries. That sport of mine, a simple game, would take on unreal proportions. How could the mere sight of me cause such violent reactions in those people? Whenever I went into Marseille, things would hot up; on the motorway I'd see people almost cause accidents, just to catch a glimpse of me, to wave at me, to try and stop me. I'd get thank-you letters: 'Well done for everything you do for OM.' I loved this passion but it got too much for me eventually. After our victory against Newcastle and my two goals, I got grumpy because I couldn't understand how people could just stare at me so wide-eyed. I had a hard time accepting it; I was just a footballer. Then I understood that I couldn't stay there in my bubble; those things that were happening to me were what I'd wanted and I just had to deal with them. It was harder for Kévin to make friends at school because he was Drogba's son. He didn't know who he was any more, questioned the motives of kids his own age.

My status had exceeded my powers. I'd gone to the bedside of a kid who had cancer but it was too much for me . . . I never did it again. The days after that, I felt bad, I couldn't accept this situation and it had shaken me. Maybe I wasn't strong enough to face the challenges life was throwing at me, even though I knew how much some troubled children liked me and longed to meet me . . .

Eventually, along my many travels, I got to understand Marseille's impact on the world; this club really has its own identity. I saw OM shirts in the United States, as well as in small-town markets. In Africa too, of course. This club has a huge potential in terms of merchandising, just like Barcelona, Manchester, Chelsea or Milan. Even in Abidjan there's a café with OM's colours in zone 4, where the hottest nightlife is. Oh, Marseille!

What a joy at any rate to live in that sun-drenched region. We'd originally moved to the Aubagne area, then to La Ciotat. We'd have coffee on the terrace in the middle of December, we felt right at home.

The way I see it, a club is a unit made up of a team, a public, a city, a relationship. Even after I'd left, I rang up José Anigo the coach before he left, to tell him to hang in there; I just couldn't ignore his problems, those troubles at the top. I had everything it took to live out my sport in Marseille. Sadly, I wasn't able to stay as long as I would have liked to.

8

TREASON

It was a passing remark made by a Marseille journalist as I was coming out of a press conference:

– Have you heard the latest? It seems an English club has made OM an offer. I don't know which club, but I'll let you know if I find out.

– It's not important. Don't bother looking. There's no way I'm going anywhere.

Not in my second year anyway, maybe a little later. When I was little, my friends and I often talked about foreign clubs like they were the greatest thing on earth. But I wasn't really desperate to go any more. Marseille had brought me happiness, excitement, passion. What could lure me away now? I was like a king on his throne, just without the crown.

Why would I leave my comfortable position? It wasn't going to happen.

I learned the name of the club in question, it was Chelsea. My friend called: 'So, they want you for 20 million! . . . What is this club? Forget it.' It was almost a joke. I didn't want to go anywhere. The only team that could have made me think twice was AC Milan, because of what that club represented in my imagination.

Even though I know that Ariedo Braida, their director-general, liked me, no serious contact had been made, but that wasn't important.

Pape Diouf had become OM's general manager and we were already working on the next season. I had discussed things with José Anigo and was taken into their confidence about signings. So there was no reason to be worried; the club wanted to give me the best possible sporting conditions. There were debates like: 'I prefer such and such a player because he's more of an all-rounder, he'll be of more use up front . . .' I was in tune with the management and supporters, my financial terms had just been reassessed and my contract extended five years. So there was no reason to think about going anywhere else. I was more focused on building a competitive team to get the championship title, to finally break Lyon's stranglehold. It was quite a challenge. I had also set myself another personal aim: beat the record of goals scored in a single season held by Jean-Pierre Papin: 30. We were going to keep Camel Meriem, a great passer, and strengthen the midfield. I spoke to Benoît Pedretti, the Sochaux midfielder, on the phone and insisted he join the team. 'You'll see, it'll be great. We'll get on really well. We have everything we need here to succeed.' We were also after Mario Yepes, really the top men at the time. In full flight, the Colombian could have broken through anything, tackling Mozer or Boli in the centre of the field. He was pure style and would set Marseille on fire. We had also thought about Marcelo Gallardo, the amazing Argentinian technician, who had spent time at Monaco. He had the right style for the Vélodrome. A solid, creative and powerful signing; an ambitious signing.

I flew to Cameroon with the Ivory Coast team feeling calm. We were going to play a very important game there in the qualification round for the African Cup of Nations and the 2006 World Cup. While I was there journalists kept going over this story about me leaving. There were offers, of course, but I wasn't worried. After all, nothing could happen to me while everyone was counting on me.

After the match against the Lions Indomptables (2–0), Pape Diouf called me in my hotel room. Solemn moment. He had arrived before the match, but, strangely, hadn't wanted to interrupt my preparations. 'They've accepted Chelsea's offer. The club is ready to sell you.' It was like taking one right in the face from Mike Tyson. KO. The first thing I said after I pulled myself together was 'I don't want to leave, so I'm not going.' But Pape added, 'It's all ready. The chairman has thought over the offer. He's given his OK.' I went nuts. My world was caving in. How could OM have accepted this deal behind my back? Pape spoke again: 'As a former agent, I should tell you that you can't refuse this offer, because you're going to be able to look after your family for the rest of your days.' So?

I wasn't ready to listen. 'Pape, money doesn't guide my decisions. We're happy with what we have. Tell the chairman to give me half what Chelsea are offering net as gross at Marseille and I'll stay. That's enough for me. I couldn't care less about this offer, call the chairman.'

He told me to think it over. Dagui Bakari, my room-mate with the Ivory Coast team, found it hard to understand my anger. 'What's wrong with you? You have to go! It's a huge opportunity that won't come round again.'

I probably wasn't being objective, I was speaking from my heart. It was a terrible decision to have to take. My wife couldn't help me because I wasn't going to her with a club I wanted to go to. What argument could I use to go into exile? I was totally confused. I called José Anigo, my coach. 'José, what the hell's going on?' Answer: 'I can't say anything.' He must have been disappointed too. He had told everybody he was going to build a team around me.

Then I got Christophe Bouchet on the phone. 'Mr Chairman, I'm not thinking irrationally.' My seduction operation had begun. He tried to convince me that this departure was a good idea. Both for me and OM. It was the same arguments over and over again. Thierno, my agent, loyalest of the loyals, saw things exactly the same way. 'From the start of your career, you've not had lots of money. You can't let this chance slip past. You can't. Think about your future. Other stars have come through OM, but when their careers came to an end they were forgotten. Skoblar, Magnusson . . . They're still talked about, of course, and those of us who knew them may even shake their hands. But what happens afterwards? You weren't programmed to be a star. Thinking as your adviser, you can increase your salary several times over, you're crazy if you don't go. Looking at where you've come from, you can't turn your nose up at this. When I think of all the old players squatting in the wings of clubs, trying to earn a little money . . . You're going to Chelsea!' He called my wife to insist. Everyone was ganging up against what I wanted.

I saw this wish to sell me as Marseille and the chairman betraying me. In a way, reading between the lines, this decision was saying that I couldn't keep up my last year's level. A little like Van Buyten, the Belgian defender who was sent to Germany. OM was going to get whatever money they could for me, that was enough.

It was a clever way of not giving me their full trust despite the fine words.

Still, I was touched that José Mourinho, the Portuguese manager, wanted me that much. He was charismatic and I had a good feeling about him. I met with the management of the English club in Paris when I got back from Cameroon and I made an agreement with them, despite what I was feeling inside. After the meeting with my future employers, I went home. Chelsea were going to sign me. When I had the medical check-up in the French capital I longed for them to find some sort of problem. A damaged knee or a bad ankle . . . They weren't going to buy a guy in that sort of shape! I wasn't ready to go.

It was that day that I understood football is a business. Of course, I could have refused, but the club's desire to sell me was too strong. Feeling more comfortable with the situation, I went over the reasons the OM staff had given me in my head: 'It's better for you; you're going to a great club; your departure will allow us to have a formidable team next year with good players, even if they aren't as good as you.' I really didn't care about their arguments. Once I saw their minds were made up, I said OK. Let's go to Chelsea. I had no contact with the main shareholder Robert Louis-Dreyfus during this time.

My reaction may seem over the top, surprising to some people. But I had my way of thinking. I didn't grow up in a 'money at all costs' culture and I'm attached to notions of family. We were OM, a group, united. There was solidarity among us. Money shouldn't be a part of that kind of relationship, it shouldn't interfere with perfect happiness. So I felt like I'd had a smack in the mouth.

I finally decided against all of these arguments. If the club was so determined to sell me, why should I be the only one objecting? So I accepted the offer. Around 37 million euros for OM, not for me, obviously . . . The largest transfer at the time! Pape Diouf and Christophe Bouchet told me they had declined Juve and AC Milan's offers, which were lower by half.

*

I had tears in my eyes during the goodbye press conference at OM. I was leaving for a big club with my head held low, a funny image. I didn't know what to say to the Marseille fans in my remarks at the event organised at the Vélodrome. I mumbled some appropriate words. 'This chance to go to Chelsea is in very large part thanks to OM. I'm going with a heavy heart. My mind was made up by the fact that a coach like Mourinho is interested in having me, that he's counting on me and wants to build a team round me. I'm looking forward to living a new and exciting adventure at Chelsea, which is a great club. It makes the decision less painful. There are also financial reasons, and I'd be lying if I left those aspects out. Chelsea's offer just can't be refused, either by OM or myself.'

I recited the arguments that had been repeated to me over and over again. At least I finished the conference with my truth: 'Go OM!' That crack was pure Drogba. Deep down in my guts. I said it sitting next to Christophe Bouchet, the man who'd sold me.

After the conference, I went back to the empty dressing room. The heart of my home territory, my cocoon. I was ranting at them in my head, I was really mad at Bouchet, the chairman. I picked up my locker plate with the number 11 and my name, 'Drogba Didier'. It was a souvenir that I didn't want to leave behind. I walked out onto the ground one last time. The stadium was deserted. I was angry at myself for not saying goodbye to those wonderful fans, for not having been with them one last time. Tears brimmed up. I felt weak and my heart was tied in knots. I began sobbing, alone in the middle of the lifeless pitch that seemed to lack spirit. I was alone in my negative thoughts. Alone with myself. Then I took my car and went down to the coast. The Mediterranean stretched out as far as the eye could see; just the water and my blues, my sadness. I stayed for about an hour, I felt terrible. That's the way it happened. No offence, but Chelsea didn't mean a whole lot in France. It didn't mean much to me. I watched their Champions League match with Monaco. I was on Monaco's side. I knew Deschamps, Desailly, Makelele, Zola, I knew they were great footballers. But it wasn't my team. It wasn't my OM. I just didn't have any desire to be part of that team.

The day before leaving for Chelsea, when I had to sign the final contract, I didn't go to get Thierno from the airport. It was too hard. I didn't feel myself. I had the feeling I was being chased out of OM despite the fact I'd given my all to the club; all my strength, all of my willpower. I had played when I was tired, when I was injured, but I'd always given my best, without holding anything back. But I'd become a mere piece of merchandise to be traded. There was no connection now between my personal feelings and my professional life.

It was around 10 p.m. when Thierno arrived at the house. I had spent some time at one of my friends' places. I was unhappy. 'Something wrong, kid?' Thierno asked. 'I'm fine, fine . . .' The TV was showing the press conference on a loop. It was too hard to watch it. I was on the verge of tears, I felt lost in my own home. It was a turning point in my life as a sportsman, as a man, and my own wishes had little to do with it. Lalla was packing the bags. Pascal, who I'll speak of later, was there. The kids too.

Thierno lay down on the sofa because we had to get up at 6 a.m. Obviously, I didn't get a wink's sleep all night. Around 4 a.m. I came downstairs. I'd changed my mind. After all, the final decision was mine. 'Thierno, I'm not going to Chelsea!' His answer was dry. I understood that he didn't want to go over it again. 'Why? Go to bed.' 'No, you don't understand. I don't want to go.'

'I don't want to get into a discussion at this hour.' We would have just gone over the same issues. The same details. What would it have achieved? What would it have changed? Nothing.

With a little smile, he said, 'Go to your room. We'll be getting up soon.' Did he really believe I was going to be able to sleep?

We ran into Jean Tigana on the plane to London. Diouf, the OM general manager, was no longer my agent. So I was accompanied by Thierno and Pierre Frelot, the man who had succeeded Diouf at the head of the set-up. We left Marseille at 7 a.m. as the summer heat began to rise. I was wearing a white V-neck T-shirt, I hadn't even taken a jacket. Peter Kenyon, the executive director, came to meet us. It was freezing up there.

It was all pretty drab. We ran into congestion. The grey of the sky was getting to my head. We arrived at the Chelsea Village and David Barnard, the secretary general, and Kenyon were waiting for us. But the chairman, Roman Abramovich, wasn't. Pape was there from the Marseille side, he looked at us, shook our hands. It was funny. Pape was on the other side of the barrier, he picked up his stuff, and as he left said 'Good luck son, good deal.' He gave me a few pieces of advice. He really knew business. We debated everything, point by point. We went for lunch around midday. Not a single manager came with us. Thierno would later admit to me that he was having some doubts right then. 'What sort of club am I sending this guy to? It was the world's largest transfer ever and no one came with us! Nobody took much notice.' He didn't want to talk to me about it. He was scared of plunging me even further into that feeling of helplessness.

We signed the contract and I went to pick up my strip. I wanted the number 11, but Damien Duff had it. There was no question of taking it off him. Number 15, the day my son Isaac was born, was free. A photo, a smile, a brief interview. I went to my suite in the Chelsea hotel in the shadow of Stamford Bridge. I watched Thierno leave . . . I was feeling sad. I took my things up to the room. It felt like I was going through a break-up. It was hard to say goodbye. I gave him a hug. A few standard words of encouragement, then we tried to avoid looking each other in the eye . . . I was like a child being torn from his parents on the first day of school. I felt alone and abandoned.

I was on my own in the hotel room. I felt depressed. It was a horrible night. Luckily, in the morning the bus came to take me to the training centre close to Heathrow. Geremi and three or four of the other players were already sat on the bus. As I got on board my Cameroonian friend shouted, 'Welcome and congratulations. We Blacks are happy, proud to have someone here who represents us.' These words were soothing. He had managed to find those comforting phrases, those phrases you wait to hear. When we got to where we were going, I saw Gallas and Makelele and I began to get my head out of the water a little.

I was busy, and so less buried in my dark thoughts.

Among all the other things we had to do, we had the departure to the US for the traditional pre-season tournament. The flight seemed painful and long. When I saw the size of the plane we had rented I couldn't believe it! 'What kind of club is this?!' I took the same sort of plane to fly to Abidjan. This was just a football team going away for a tournament, a club with enormous resources. I got depressed during the journey. They were difficult feelings to shed. I looked at the faces around me, the faces that were going to escort me through my London journey. I looked at the stars like John Terry and Frank Lampard who I didn't really know. Chelsea weren't that much in the news in France, as I said, even though the Euro Championship had given me a glimpse of these Blues playing for England against France, at the beginning of the tournament in Portugal. We spoke about them before the match, I watched them closely. And they watched me.

I was deep in my thoughts. I could only imagine the shape of that future OM being drawn up somewhere offstage. Sure, we would have achieved something huge. I would have forced certain things and put pressure on the management to get it done. Maybe they felt it coming and preferred to see me go elsewhere . . . I'm not going to bear a grudge for life. I saw Bouchet again . . . He hurt me so much that year! I was so pissed at him. Honestly. Really, really angry. My dream had been destroyed. I was so looking forward to being champion with OM. I was preparing for it. The team was beginning to form. I was going to take a month's holiday and we'd see what we would see. We saw. First and foremost, we saw me with a Chelsea shirt on.

I couldn't just wave a magic wand and be done with Marseille. That would have been impossible. Nostalgia was holding me back. When I had free time, I would go down there, but it was hard with players like Péguy Luyindula who had problems with it. People recognised me. It wasn't a good thing to hear the stadium chant my name as my replacements were taking the field. I had to cut the umbilical cord. My time at OM had come to an end after just a year, but it felt like I'd been there for ever. I'd had a vision of complete loyalty, of belonging to a club, to a jersey, like Paolo Maldini, the model for all the other models. Him and Milan. Drogba and Marseille, it even had a nice ring to it. That idea only lived in my dreams. I was disgusted at having to sign for Chelsea. That may seem strange. But that's how I felt.

9

THE £24 MILLION MAN

My life in England began in the US during a tour. Same language, same sadness. I was lost, and would be for a long time, a very long time . . . That first season was truly hard to manage. With a difficult label to bear: the man worth £24 million. €37 million. I was no longer Didier Drogba, I was an astronomical amount of money tacked on to my name whenever something didn't go perfectly, whenever I missed a chance, whenever I lost my balance . . .

How could I explain that I didn't deserve that nickname? That money didn't go into my pocket. It went from London to Marseille. I was the same boy Guingamp bought from Le Mans for €150,000 and who OM bought for €6 million a year and a half later. If José Mourinho had bought me for that price, he must have thought I was worth it, or at least that the club could afford it to secure my services. That was enough for me. It was obviously not enough for everyone.

I don't want to get into pointless arguments about transfer prices, or footballers' well-earned bank accounts, especially in England: it's never been about money for me, and my history proves it has never got in the way of my beliefs. Was I going to refuse what I was being offered? Obviously not. The player is just a link in the chain. The system is bigger than him but he can make use of it just as the clubs make use of him through merchandising. It's a give–give, win–win situation.

Nevertheless, those £24 million led to jealousy, even among the squad. It's not easy to walk into a dressing room with that figure hanging around your neck.

At the beginning, I felt that I wasn't welcomed by the English players, wasn't accepted. I was the new guy, I couldn't speak the language, I couldn't really understand their jokes, that special British humour. The language barrier really bothered me. The others were all used to working as a team and I had the impression that they weren't playing with me. I felt a separation between the English and everyone else during training. I was the foreigner that people avoided. Fortunately, apart from the French-speakers, some others, such as the Portuguese players Tiago and Paulo Ferreira, spoke my language too. Mateja Kežman and Arjen Robben, the two Dutch players, also understood a little. So did the Russian Alexei Smertin, who had spent time with Bordeaux. They helped me adapt.

Obviously, this situation wasn't easy to understand. It took me some time to get it, to accept their attitude.

I realised their differences because of that distance. In the end, they all turned out completely normal. Everyone fell into a group of people like themselves, often linked to nationality or a shared past. Before arriving at Chelsea, I used to hang out with my teammates, I thrived on team life. Not here. That's why I was so surprised, and it affected me for quite a while. Makelele and Gallas, who were more mature and had travelled more, kept repeating, 'That's the way things are. These differences are normal.' The blacks go with the other blacks, Portuguese with Portuguese, English with English. You had to find your place, your own balance, that's all.

Only results solidify a team and make it stronger. Everything else is just words. This also came out in the structure of our dressing rooms at training: Terry is close to Lampard, those that come from Africa are neighbours.

Geremi, my great mate, often repeated: 'Forget the sea and the sun. That's all done! You have to wake up or you'll regret it.' Gallas was also fed up that I kept going back over my year in Marseille. He even gave me a slap, as if that were the end of it. 'If you keep going like this, you'll be making a mistake!' It wasn't clear to me, but he was right. We don't grow through memories. They only enrich an existence, a career, in retrospect.

The other annoyance I had was due to the British media: they didn't know me. My pride took a hit. I thought that my performances in the UEFA Cup and in the Champions League would have been enough to gain a small reputation. I was wrong. Nothing at all, or almost nothing. Here, the striker with 11 goals on the Continent didn't even exist. Still, I was selected as number one in Ligue 1 by my peers, and clubs of the calibre of Juve and AC Milan had been interested in me. My name had also been touted in Spain. That's not nothing, you know? But they didn't rate me in England. Apart from my transfer I was ignored. I just didn't get it.

Perhaps I was also brought into a team that hadn't yet won its stripes. The club was being run by a Russian billionaire, Roman Abramovich, and it played against 'real' English clubs like Sir Alex Ferguson's Manchester United or Arsène Wenger's Arsenal, a man who over time had almost come to be considered English.

The elegant Frenchman carried a sort of natural class and had won people's deserved respect over the years. Wasn't he called 'Arsène Who?' when he arrived from Japan? He had to prove himself in England, fight people's preconceptions and win. Always win. So I had to score. Always score.

Chelsea wanted to take a place at the national table and leave behind the narrow image of a swanky part of London. They had *nouveau riche* ambitions and market prices became Abramovich prices. Quite a change. In the eyes of many, including numerous journalists, the club was setting itself up as the club to beat, to knock down. Nevertheless, this colossal investment had been carefully thought through. Mourinho had taken on new players as part of his search for recognition. We all had something to prove.

I understood all of these changes happening to our world during our pre-season trip to the USA. I can still see myself with my trainers on the pitch, ready to do a little jogging, my twenty-, thirty-minute warm-up for my openers. Mourinho asked me: 'Didier, what are you doing? We're not training for the marathon here, we've come to play football. It's not the Olympics. Get your studs and let's go. Put your trainers away. You're not going to need them with me.'

That's when I discovered some of Mourinho's ways of working. No jogging. All our preparation would involve a ball and be on a football pitch. That surprise didn't stop me suffering physically. But our return was well planned, very enjoyable and intense. We were staying in a university and using American footballers' facilities. You can just imagine: huge dressing rooms, the guys wore sizes 12 or 13 in a shoe. Straight away I thought: 'This guy Mourinho is quite something.'

When he gave us his talk before the championship began, he was crystal-clear: 'You've never won anything, I've just come out of a successful Champions League run with Porto. Apart from Geremi, Paulo Ferreira, Ricardo Carvalho, Makelele, my staff and myself, none of you have won a title. I hope you can win one. But it's very hard to get there. It will take a group that works together, that wants to win together. OK, last year, John Terry was captain. Is it a problem if we give it back to him? No. OK, so he'll keep the armband. Let's go!' A brief exchange that was enough to plunge us into the unique world of the Premier League. He certainly didn't want anyone acting like a star. We listened to him. We had to. He was so different from the way things were in France with Marseille and Guingamp!

It was such a shock. The players trained as physically as they played in games. They were focused on each part of their work.

Even the coach had a style all his own: between two exercises he would laugh, give us hugs. But when we were 'working', the smiles would disappear. No relaxation. Maximum concentration.

These discoveries didn't stop me feeling homesick. I was suffering from a broken heart and had only had seven days' holiday. And what a holiday it was! A week spent reflecting on my situation: should I leave or not? Should I go or not?

I was tired emotionally and the coach understood that. I explained how I felt, and he put me at ease straight away. That was the first time I found a coach who was so willing to listen. Before the series of friendlies, he even told me, 'It's up to you. How long do you want to play? An hour? Fifteen minutes? You decide. You know yourself best. You're best placed to know what to do before a season in order to start on top form.' It was amazing. I played one half against Rome and scored a goal. I got the man of the match title as well as a trophy, a sort of mini-replica of the World Cup in glass. A good omen for the future? I was happy. My first goal. My first press conference in English. Well, there were better people to listen to . . . Let's say that I managed to say a few words. Our last outing in the USA before coming home was against AC Milan, one of my favourite teams. I marked Paolo Maldini at a corner. A good kick of the ball. I wanted to get Maldini's shirt, but it was too late. I got Christian Brocchi's in the end.

With the trip finished we came home with our feet on the ground. Back to London. I was thrown back into problems linked to my status as an expatriate. Chelsea didn't necessarily help me at the time. In France, even in smaller clubs, we're used to having a support structure. So at Lyon, an interpreter takes care of the Brazilians, helps them find a place to stay, to find their way about, trying to reduce the negative side of the move as much as possible. A player who is happy and at ease with himself feels comfortable on the pitch more quickly. It's not a question of needing help 24/7, that's not my style, but finding short cuts to family well-being. Even in a team of Chelsea's calibre that doesn't exist. The only person who could have helped me take care of my problems was Gary Stecker, a great guy, a sort of steward dedicated to the Blues. But he didn't have enough time to devote to us because of his many responsibilities.

The club should have put a structure in place to help the kids, the families, to adjust more quickly, because I was getting really bored in the hotel and my house-hunting was going nowhere. Chelsea sent a lady to see me, but she wanted to sell me a house for £10 million! Only because she would get a commission, I think . . . She must have thought that, given my transfer fee, I could afford it – without stopping to think that that money wasn't mine. It was a way of picking my pocket. There came a time when I said stop! I managed on my own. My search was a hard slog, largely because of my imperfect English. I had to find a place near the training centre and near an international school, so that my kids had the best chances of doing well. Finally, after weeks of disappointment, I unearthed the right place.

It was then that I remembered what Pape Diouf once said. I had just told him how much I loved the Milan clubs and my surprise at seeing that Inter's dressing rooms were almost as bad as those of a Division d'Honneur club in France (like the lower divisions in England). He responded: 'No club is perfect. There are always good things and bad. Things that should be changed, others kept the same.' He was right, but my limited experience hadn't shown me this balanced picture. I realised there were good points at Chelsea and others that were less good. So? All the new guys went through the same situation. Should I be the one to grumble? We sometimes laughed about it with Gallas, Makelele, Kežman and Geremi. 'You too? You're still living at the hotel? That's nuts! It's been a month and a half and you've still not got somewhere to live!' If I'd been the only one in that situation I might have let it get to me, but that wasn't the case.

With all these worries, I didn't feel like integrating, making more of an effort. That made it difficult to avoid injuries.

So I wasn't spared anything in my first season. I faced three different setbacks: more than a month out due to an inguinal hernia, three weeks because of a detached aponeurosis and as many again because of a knee problem.

I've often played through pain that harmed my performance. I would read the sports pages of the newspapers: 'He's having problems adjusting to his transfer!' Nope, I was having problems with my body. I couldn't care less about how much my transfer fee had been.

I wasn't necessarily noticed in the dressing room either. I was the guy who'd come along to take Eider Gudjohnsen's job – and he was a mate of the senior players. It took a while to show them that wasn't what I was aiming to do. I was there to compensate for Hernán Crespo's departure, not to steal the Icelander's position. There was a slot available. Kežman, another striker, didn't play a lot, and only had an OK time. His relations with the coach were chilly.

In any case, I saw Gudjohnsen as one of the greats. From my arrival, he was one of the people who left the greatest impression. Technically, he could do anything. His control of the ball was exceptional and his speed only improved his natural skills.

Other players had amazed me at the start and gone on to confirm it during the season:

– Frank Lampard: a top-flight player. Very, very, very good. He also had a staggering ability to play match after match without stopping. He never listened, he would go beyond the pain. He had enormous drive.

– John Terry: a mental monster. He was 24 when I arrived and he was already the captain. That distinction means a lot in a club of Chelsea's quality. He had charisma, a high status, and above all, he was able to get his head places where I couldn't get my foot. Even if he got hit, he would pick himself back up and get back to work. Sometimes I would say to him: 'John, you're either crazy or you're not thinking straight. You're OK right now, but think of your future.' That attitude always worked. A real mental fighter.

– Claude Makelele: I often used to watch him on TV. His years at Real had turned him into Zinédine Zidane's essential companion, the player who kept the star safe. I didn't know just how strong he was, both technically and physically. We saw him as fragile, almost frail, but he never gave up in one-on-ones. He always won those physical duels. His placement was intelligent, he had a crazy sort of charisma with his colleagues and he was the essential element that year.

– William Gallas: He was also one of the 'impassables'. For him to lose a duel he had to be having a bad day, be tired, or not feel like training. I saw each striker break against him like a wave on the rocks. Unsinkable William.

I was a lot less so. Of course, I had intensely happy moments during that English baptism, such as the League Cup final we won in Cardiff against Liverpool. There was something magical about that drawn-out success in February 2005 (3–2). I was crazy with joy when the final whistle blew. I had scored and I felt I was an essential pawn in the Mourinho system in a very specific role. In fact, I wanted to make up for my mistake against Barcelona where I was sent off when we were leading

1–0 before losing two goals in the Nou Camp away in the last sixteen of the Champions League. I owed that trophy to the club, to my coach, to my teammates. I had got them in trouble in the Champions League. That sending-off really affected me. I kept my position in the starting line-up against Liverpool in the next match; Mourinho had shown me a certain respect that I absolutely had to justify. To cap it all, it was my first title. I must have won a cup when I was nine or ten in Abbeville or Dunkirk, but since then I'd been in the desert.

This success in the League Cup was also proof of what I could do, despite the criticism. But that joy was still not enough to clear up my blues, my homesickness, my longing for Marseille. You don't bring a love story to an end without leaving a bit of your heart behind. I'd watch videos that OM fans made for me with longing. I'd look back at myself wearing the jersey, my face splitting open with joy, with the music playing again . . .

I even really believed that I would return. I met Robert Louis-Dreyfus, the OM majority shareholder, the owner, in his London offices. Then we went to eat in a French restaurant. He tried to see how they could perhaps get me back. We discussed it. I was so angry. Then he explained to me how the transfer had gone, the underlying reasons for my departure. I listened. Did I understand? Not really. It wasn't really worth going over a hurtful past, but my case seemed complicated. Even now it would be difficult for me to repeat what RLD said . . . In any event, I moved on to something else. I was depressed, no doubt about it. I let my bleeding heart speak. I went through all the things that got on my nerves. It gets dark between 3 and 4 p.m., the shops close early, sometimes at 5 or 6. We weren't used to it and my children and wife weren't happy. When Isaac, who was three and a half, came to see me to say 'Dad, I want to go back,' it turned me upside down. What he wanted was what I wanted, the entire Drogba family were on the same wavelength. RLD to the rescue?

During our meal I realised that he knew all there was to know about football. It was the first time I had spoken with him for more than five minutes, and that's what I discovered. He had near-encyclopedic knowledge. He had tapes on players, went to see all the big matches. He would have been the perfect recruiter, I'm sure of it. Robert Louis-Dreyfus spoke about football without making a single slip. He allowed me a glimpse of returning to my city. I believed him; I clung to that hope like a drowning man to his lifejacket. That's no exaggeration.

The second interview, however, was less productive. 'It may be possible to bring you back, but we'd have to see if Chelsea will agree first. How much will the management want to let you leave? Or we could try and organise a loan.' That was out of the question in my opinion.

— If I go back to Marseille, it will be through a transfer, not a loan.

— We can't manage that at the moment. We'll see where we finish in the league. If we qualify for the European Cup, we could consider a transfer then.

– OK. Anyway, the ball is in your court. I'm ready to come back.

He then added that everything was down to how Marseille fared in the Cup and the championship. I realised then that my future depended too much on rain or shine. I said: 'It's not worth it. Let's leave things as they are.' I'd have to make an impression with the Blues, and get over my depression.

Also, I had to get back to full physical fitness because my injuries had really taken their toll. When I look back on my stats, they were quite good before that damned hernia. After the operation, I'd lost the use of my abdominals. There was nothing left. I couldn't even raise my legs 10 centimetres off the ground when I was lying on my back; that simple exercise, which everyone can do at the foot of their bed in the morning, was my Mount Everest. My medical monitoring, which I'll speak of later, helped me speed up my recovery and I healed more quickly than anticipated.

Within the group, links were forged and country hotels rang with the noise of Makelele, Geremi, Gallas's and my poker parties. They brightened up our trips, and managed to clear up my blues a little. So everything wasn't that bad.

By the end of my first year we were champions of England and League Cup winners: two trophies in my new cabinet. But I didn't really take any pleasure from either of them. We also managed to push through to the Champions League semi-final, where we were knocked out by Liverpool, an old acquaintance. Despite this convincing CV, I wanted to leave.

Happiness doesn't come from results, it comes from well-being. And an absolutely crucial fact: my relationship with the fans wasn't close. I had always defined myself through my strong and deep relations with the fans, so that really undermined me. Even after my first few goals at Guingamp, I went towards the stands to thank them.

Blues season ticket-holders were expecting a big name. I was no Shevchenko or Ronaldo, the stars whose names had been mentioned when Crespo left. So a player from the Ivory Coast who'd been playing in France . . . I wasn't the unanimous choice, that's for sure. Furthermore, the way they used me stopped me from playing at my best. I gave my all to achieve the club's objectives. I fought for the team, for everyone. I'd think to myself that the game depended on me, and spend a little less time running in all directions. I made sacrifices. I had to think in terms of the trophy, not goals. In the end I finished well behind Thierry Henry in terms of goals scored (10 against 25) and I can't say I was exactly thrilled about that . . .

The press saw me as a control tower, a big workhorse who was there to send the ball to others with his head and to open up spaces. Not really very fulfilling. In their eyes, I was a clumsy guy who didn't score very often. I didn't like that image at all. I also had trouble adapting to the rhythm of the game, the power of the hits, the impacts.

In France, we listen to each other a lot, we try to spare our bodies. Not in England. Here, I could see guys suffering but not pulling out because of minor details like that. I would often hear: 'I'm playing through the pain.' I understood a lot, especially the power that mental strength can have over performances and freshness. In France, playing three consecutive matches in a week creates strains. The chairmen complain, the coaches follow. 'That's unacceptable, how can we take that? We're going to burn the guys out.' Inevitably, that means the players can always find excuses when they're momentarily tired. None of that in England. It would be shameful to abandon ship, to not feel up to going back out on the pitch two days after a match. We take on the mantles of warriors.

When I arrived, we had three matches scheduled in one week at the end of August. I thought: 'I'm never going to handle this pace. It's impossible.' That was typical French reasoning. Once you get on the pitch, in that special scene, with the other guys around you, all you can think about is getting stuck in. You blank out those criticisms of matches too close together. Obviously this crazy schedule penalises teams that don't have a large pool of players, and it makes sense to see the big teams clear up over the Christmas period when the matches come thick and fast. But even players at lesser teams run like it was the first match of the Premier League season. It's all a question of attitude.

And Christmas was another novelty. When I saw those nuts cram into the stands during the winter holidays, I just couldn't get over it. Entire families in a really festive atmosphere. I should say that I wasn't exactly looking forward to that period with any great glee.

For my first New Year's Eve in the country, I was treated to playing Liverpool the next day! My telephone rang at midnight. My friends were calling to wish me a happy new year. Swines! They took advantage of the situation to have a little drink. We were getting ready for a clash with the favourites. We won (1–0) at Anfield, almost at lunchtime. The title may actually have been won with four consecutive victories in eight days in the middle of the winter period. I even scored the two winning goals against Middlesbrough (2–0).

It's worth noting that it was at this time that I discovered this country's passion for the game. It's a real religion, like in Africa. Full stadiums, loving stares; I saw kids and their parents filling the streets. It's beautiful to see football at the centre of a country's culture.

When I think back to those beginnings, to that year when I was just learning the ropes, to that championship title, I realise that I couldn't have left, in spite of wanting to.

I would have missed those unexpected feelings. Taking a step back always helps to put things in perspective. I couldn't leave this club in semi-failure. Understand and learn about England, its championship, its quirks . . . I just had to do it in order to grow. Even through pain . . .

10

'SOMETIMES I DIVE . . .'

Nothing has ever been easy for me. During my second season I realised that even more in my relationship with the supporters. It was a major crisis. Yet having scored two goals against Manchester City, there was no obvious reason for me to fall out with the fans. It was 25 March 2006.

With my first year under my belt, I was ready to show another side of my nature. Frankly, on a personal level, the holidays had refreshed me. The language barrier was becoming less of a problem. I managed a double against Arsenal (2–1) in the Community Shield, the first game of the season at the beginning of August against the reigning Cup winners. We couldn't have dreamt of a better start.

With Hernán Crespo, the Argentinian who nearly went to AC Milan, with me, it was like having extra strength in my legs. But I didn't really see his arrival as competition. Above all, over time, I aimed to build a partnership with him up front. He's a good guy, and what's more, a great footballer. He's really cunning on the pitch, he can just sense the ball and always gets into the perfect position. We had to give Mourinho a bit of a shake. He was keen to stick to his 4-3-3, but that formation allowed for only one striker: Crespo or me. When one of us scored he would hold on to his starting position for the next game. If not, the other would start.

The merry-go-round lasted until I was more often chosen than Crespo. But when we were both in the line-up, we were match-winners. All we had to do was convince the coach, which we managed over the season. I was really tired when I came back from the African Nations Cup, which was held in Egypt in February 2006. On top of that, we'd been knocked out in the last sixteen of the Champions League – by Barcelona. The Catalans were better. I went to see the coach to tell him I should sit the game out. I was tired from working in this one-striker system. We ended up trying the 4-4-2. Mourinho listened to me and put Crespo and me on the pitch. We got stuck in. He was my ideal partner.

But then came that famous match against Manchester City on 25 March 2006. A date that I'll never forget, and a precious memory. The pre-match had already thrown up serious criticism of the way I played. The English media thought I dived too much. Far too much.

We'd lost to Fulham (1–0) in the previous game. One of my teammates threw the ball in very deep and I had to go one-on-one with the goalkeeper. With the position I was in, it would have been impossible for the referee to see that I touched the ball with my hand to set it up for a goal.

The only real witnesses were the TV cameras and the spectators on that side. So, the referee gave the goal before changing his mind. Why? The Fulham players had protested, along with the screaming and gesticulating fans. The fourth official must have seen my hand on tape although that couldn't, and still can't, be used. Later, Raymond Domenech would be involved in the world's first video decision during the World Cup final after Zidane was sent off for head-butting Marco Materazzi. I had fallen victim to this electronic judgment myself not long before.

That decision caused a major controversy before the Manchester City match. The match would only rekindle the tension and the controversy that surrounded me . . . The ball was flighted towards my hand off a corner kick, and my reflex was to use my arm. That allowed me to take control and hit it on the half-volley. A very nice goal. But Sylvain Distin saw the foul and protested, leading to a second yellow card, meaning a sending-off for him. A few minutes later, I upped the ante with a move they couldn't match, after taking the ball from David Sommeil and leaving him in my wake.

In the second half, I set off on a counter-attack, but while I was trying to get past Richard Dunne, the Manchester defender stuck his finger in my eye. I stopped in my tracks and fell down on the pitch. I wasn't trying to get a penalty. It just hurt. All of a sudden, a deafening noise came crashing down from the stands: I was being booed by some Chelsea fans too! My own supporters! They hadn't seen the foul, but they already seemed to be fingering my attitude. The behaviour of a cheat in their eyes. Perhaps I could have understood the opposing fans who made up an ironic chant based on my transfer fee: 'What a waste of money.' That was their job. But my own supporters . . .

Five minutes from the end of the game when I was walking round behind the goal I heard I'd been chosen man of the match. All of a sudden, when the announcement was made, quite a few of the spectators began to boo.

I blew a gasket in the dressing room. I exploded in a way I very rarely do. I screamed: 'If people aren't happy, I'll leave, I'm out of here. I'm off!' I was fit to burst. Then I went into the interview room for the press conference. On the way, a BBC journalist stopped me for a few questions. He was clearly trying to get into the controversy about diving, about the whistling.

He took advantage of my poor English to trap me. In any case, that's how I felt. The guy asked me if I'd touched the ball with my hand. Well, yeah, it was obvious. But why would I stop playing? That's what the ref is for.

Next question: 'What do you think about the people who say you're always diving?'

To which I said it happens, that's part of the game. Sometimes you have to dive because your opponent is going to hurt you. That's where the famous phrase 'sometimes I dive' came from; taken out of context in a rare moment of anger. I had scored two goals, been chosen man of the match and all I got was criticism.

I read the British press the next day: 'Yes, I'm a cheat,' says Drogba. 'Yes, I dive.' There were 89 articles on me. Quite the tribute . . . Fortunately a few people spoke up for me. In particular, Arsène Wenger defended me: 'Drogba is under the spotlight at the moment, but overall I like his attitude. He's not a cheat. He makes more of it sometimes, like many strikers do, but sometimes they are pushed by defenders when nobody sees it. Defenders also foul strikers. You shouldn't be pointing your finger.'

This advice didn't change people's perceptions. I'm not going to tell you the end of season I had. 'He's a cheat, a faker.' Whenever I got the ball people shouted and insulted me. In those moments I wasn't thinking right, I would have done anything to show them they were wrong. That attitude didn't stop me finishing on fire with three goals. I've always thrived on adversity. That was my best match of the season. The fans had got me so angry that I wanted to show them what I was made of.

Just like at the beginning of the League against Arsenal. I missed a half-volley. I saw a guy in the stand, not far from the goal, who was gesturing at me, he was giving me the finger. He was insulting me. I went to see him after I scored. 'What do you say now?' That was my revenge.

*

Even though I've always stated my desire to play elsewhere, I've always respected the Premiership, the English. So those reactions from my own fans offended me. I even said so to the Chelsea TV station: 'There's no problem. If they want me to leave all they have to do is sign a petition. And I'll get out of here. All they have to do is write to Abramovich.'

After that business, we changed the system once and for all. And it was a good thing, because it would have been harder for me to manage. Mourinho really protected me through that period. Two matches after what happened with Manchester City, I had a great game against West Ham (4–1). I won the match almost on my own. Mourinho, in his intelligent and cheerful way, whispered something to me before leaving: 'You should go home and buy all the papers tomorrow morning. Savour it.' It was sweet revenge after one of the hardest times I had at Chelsea.

That didn't mean the press cut me any slack. Looking back at a famous daily paper, their build-up for an upcoming match went: on the one hand, the man Chelsea should follow; on the other, the man they shouldn't. Who was the one they shouldn't look towards? Drogba, obviously. I learned the newspapers' game here. That doesn't stop me reading them: I like to look through them, see what they have to say. But I chose papers that seemed to be more sensible, more serious. More factual. How many times have I read words put into my mouth which I never said? You just have to get used to it.

In any event, over the course of that season I had won the trust of the management, by proving myself and thanks to the way I behaved. The players got to know me both as a person and a sportsman, and things were flowing a lot better with Terry and Lampard. The two trophies we won the year before had enabled us to break down certain barriers. My teammates knew what I brought to the table: they supported me. For them, I was no cheat. They knew there are some contacts you can't brush off, that sometimes you have to fall. In a way, my physique did me a disservice. Referees saw a big, strong guy weighing more than 90 kg and imagined to themselves: 'He can't fall!'

My build was like a handicap as people imagined that I could take more impact than others. So I had to 'add a little extra' to get the referees to blow in my favour.

Certain players who are hardly touched fall with the approval of the jury. Not me. I didn't get any favours. As if 'that big ox' wasn't human, couldn't even feel the blows. I had to work even harder to shut up those doubters.

I also played one of my best matches during that season. Against Liverpool. We won at Anfield (4–1) in October. The Reds hadn't lost at home by such a wide margin in ages. I made three decisive passes and won a penalty. My big day at Anfield. The season came to a close with a grand finale against Manchester United at Stamford Bridge (3–0). At home, it was huge, the match of the season. With victory came the title. We had played host to our strongest opponents with a six-point advantage and we had played perfectly. We couldn't have asked for better surroundings than Stamford Bridge to celebrate.

That year I finished as top passer in the club and Lampard as top scorer, with 20 goals (16 in the League). But I wasn't in competition with Frank. To be honest though, it did annoy me a little that I hadn't scored more . . . But I learned how to deal with it. He's an incredibly generous player on the pitch, a real hard worker. He always puts in so much effort: I couldn't be jealous of him, of his efficiency. I was, and I admit it, slightly frustrated. I said to myself: 'I'd score more goals if I had the ball to my feet more often.'

Lampard was smart enough to read my game perfectly just when the coach was making us progress in a quite special system. I was meant to drive through the walls, move defenders around, win physical battles. He was able to make the best of my efforts thanks to his scoring abilities, his sense of what was on. Really, well done to him! I'm not going to criticise him for taking those chances: it's a talent to have that tactical strength.

On the other hand, those feelings of being a striker gone slightly astray prevented me from taking action, from going to the coach. Finishing top passer in the league with 12 assists was not necessarily a success story. A striker likes to see the net shake. He lives for those moments of euphoria. With only 16 goals in all competitions, of which 12 were in the league, something was missing.

Nevertheless, Chelsea seemed untouchable. We felt we were feared in England, that we could inspire fear. We felt we were getting stronger and stronger, becoming almost invincible. Whenever our team was in trouble we could come back, we could count on everyone. The coach's speeches were the best. There are times in a career when everything just falls into place naturally. Sometimes, Mourinho changed his tune. We all knew our role, our obligations. And we each showed our thanks on the pitch in our own way.

It's something special when there's a Robben in the group. Of course, he wasn't the best team player over ninety minutes and you had to push him so he didn't forget you for certain moves. He wasn't the toughest fighter on the pitch either, but he could win you the game all on his own. That was his main ability. He was often injured, but when he found his form again he was explosive. The coaches often repeated: 'People are sick of him, we're going to sell him. He's always out injured.' All he had to do was come back for us to understand how indispensable he was. We needed him. An exceptional player with the ball at his feet.

But the most impressive players on the team were a magnificent trio: William Gallas, Joe Cole and Frank Lampard. While I'm not mentioning Petr Cech, who obviously had a different role, he was just as influential. Our goalkeeper soared over any debate. On the pitch, those three were the bosses. It was incredible. Cole opened up holes, unbalancing any defence.

Everyone let their feelings be known in the dressing room, John Terry, Frank, William and myself. It's a grown-up group, we weren't ones for big speeches. Just things like: 'Boys, we're in.' Did we only have to say so for the path we'd taken to run smoothly? There was no real tactical advice. More encouragement between different positions. It was a united group, we got on well together without really socialising outside the club. It wasn't a big deal. We burst out laughing every time we saw each other. Like at the Christmas Party. I couldn't even pretend to be a serious guy at those events: the alcohol ran freely. It was a time to explode, to fall about laughing. I'd never seen so much alcohol drunk. How could the guys down so much? The next day, at training, they were stiff as a board. They couldn't move at all. The first year, during one of these famous Christmas outings, I saw Robert Huth in such a state . . . Copying our defender. He was going to have quite a hangover. He stumbled in the nightclub. Two days later, he was in the starting line-up against Manchester United and had to mark Ruud van Nistelrooy. There are better Christmas presents. The Dutchman was hardly even there. Huth was too strong: he amazed me! The guys from the Premier League are really something else, even if I think it only lasts for a while. Your body gets fragile with all those free-flowing nights out.

Even so, that second season was the most successful.

But that doesn't mean that my wish to leave had disappeared. Lyon was still on my tail and had made enquiries about my future. I had maintained really good relations with Bernard Lacombe, the adviser to chairman Aulas. He had read analyses of my situation in the newspapers and he aimed to find out what I really thought. But that's normal. Professionally, it's the most logical, obvious way to go about things.

Taking advantage of the January 2002 transfer window, Drogba signed with En Avant de Guingamp to take his place in Ligue 1 football. **NATAF / L'ÉQUIPE**

Drogba celebrates with Guingamp team-mate Claude 'Coco' Michel (*right*). Quickly embraced by the club, he remembers his time there as one of great friendships and camaraderie. It was also a successful time, with Guingamp finishing seventh in the Championnat in the 2002–03 season, their highest ever position. **MARTIN / L'ÉQUIPE**

Drogba established a deep rapport with Guingamp's supporters, which was later repeated and excelled at Marseille. Here the banner reads: *Didier we love you. We miss you, but you will stay engraved on our hearts.* **BREGARDIS / L'ÉQUIPE**

Drogba and Frank Lampard celebrate his first goal in England, a header against Crystal Palace during Drogba's third appearance for Chelsea, August 2004. **GETTY IMAGES**

Crossing the Channel to join Chelsea, under the inspirational leadership of José Mourinho, led to Drogba's first championship medals, and a run of unprecedented success for his new team. *Overleaf*: Drogba and team-mates Gallas, Cech and Lampard bathe in champagne after topping the 2004–05 Premiership table. *Below, left*: Mourinho and Drogba during training; *right*: Drogba and his daughter Iman (*left*) and son Kevin (*right*) pose with the Barclays Premiership trophy at Stamford Bridge, May 2005. **GETTY IMAGES**

He told me OL would be interested if I were to leave Chelsea. Lyon is certainly a big team, but at that time I didn't want to leave Chelsea for OL. It wasn't in my career plan and I don't like to make decisions on a whim.

I always think things through first, I weigh up the pros and cons. If I wanted to leave, I had to look at all the different options. But Lyon is not Milan. The Italian club tried to get me when Andriy Shevchenko came to Chelsea, but the Londoners didn't want to let me go.

So leaving Chelsea for OL, knowing the links I had with Marseille in France, could seem underambitious. However, Milan, that would be something else. I would have been leaving a club with a certain status for one of the best in the world. That would have been totally different. The club of Baresi, van Basten, my idol, Rijkaard, Maldini . . . That's football . . . well, my own image of it anyway. The arrival of the Ukrainian was perhaps the best way for me to go in the opposite direction. After all, the fans were finally satisfied at seeing a star arrive, a recognised centre forward. I told the coach so: 'Perhaps it's time for me to go. I've brought two league titles to the club, but the fans still don't recognise and respect me like I believe I deserve.' It was the right moment to leave without creating problems and controversies.

So the management said to the coach: 'Didier wants to leave, why don't we bring back Crespo along with Shevchenko?' But the coach said: 'If you sell Didier, I need two new forwards.'

I know that, at the club at least, the men making the

decisions weren't against me leaving. It was good information to have . . .

But the person who was keeping me there, allowing me to stay, was Mourinho. We had started at the club together, climbed the ladder together. I think it was written down somewhere that we couldn't be split up. We were getting ready to take on our third year, with the Ukrainian up front.

11

MY FINEST SEASON

A true striker at last! The supporters felt that Chelsea was going to move up a gear. Ballon d'Or winner and a star among stars, Andriy Shevchenko would allow us to dominate Europe. Could there be a conflict of interest between us? Not at all. His arrival was not a problem. I knew that he was not being brought in to replace me, but to support me. Him and me up front; two players with different qualities. Before the season began, Mourinho explained to me that he wanted to sign Michael Ballack for midfield, and a centre forward so that we could work together, not be in competition. In my own way, I had long ago earned my place with the coach in the line-up, even if some fans had a different idea about the way we worked together. And the duo that I formed with Crespo had opened up attacking options for him.

Mourinho was interested in Samuel Eto'o or Carlos Tévez, from Argentina, but the chairman preferred Shevchenko. In any event, we were going to maintain the double-headed system that had worked so well. So, what to do?

Obviously, in the fans' view a new dimension would be added to Chelsea's game. I was a little put out by that way of thinking. Against Manchester City at the beginning of August, the referee blew and gave a free kick to the right of the goalkeeper. I heard the crowd chant: 'Sheva, Sheva . . .' Andriy stepped up to take the ball and place it. No, no, no, not there! Lampard, Ballack and I were in the wall. I recovered the ball, in my favourite area. The chants continued: 'Sheva, Sheva . . .' My strike scuffed the opposing goalkeeper's post. Some light booing came down from the stands . . . I thought to myself: 'Get lost!' Their idol was just above everyone else. He was the star. And I was almost just another player. That was tough to take. I couldn't accept that, it was one of those honour things. We had been champions two years running after all. It was like I wasn't even part of the equation.

But I wasn't angry at Sheva at all. It was the fans' reaction that irritated me. I think that's normal.

In fact, they weren't being malicious and I can understand their feelings. The Ukrainian had arrived with a dazzling record, nothing like my own. For years he had proven his worth in Europe's greatest arenas. He had a certain level of experience, a past that counted in his favour, but football is something you live day by day. It's not easy, even for a master of the art, to go from one league to another, one style to another, no matter how talented he is.

I could always fall back on my two titles as proof that I wasn't useless . . . Chelsea had waited fifty years to dominate the Premier League and we had taken the championship twice, not a bad show. Obviously that success wasn't all down to me, but I was at least an important part. I contributed to our attack. Hadn't I scored important goals in the League Cup and the Community Shield? I knew how much I could bring to the table.

I'd been lucky too, at the start of the 2006 season, in enjoying early success and riding the crest after that. Essential in all of this was that I had my own number back. That wasn't just a detail for me. An athlete can become attached to all sorts of symbols. For example, I always hop on my right foot before going out on the pitch. But above all else, I cared about my lucky number 11. As soon as I heard the rumours that Duff might be leaving I went to see the bursar. I warned him that no one was to touch that jersey if Duff was really leaving the club!

It was harder for Sheva in this new environment. I didn't really know what he was feeling because he was not very expressive. We had a professional relationship.

I tried to create a good rapport between the two of us because we were going to spend a year together up front. We had to build a mutual understanding. At one point, I set him up but didn't get the return I expected. I said to myself, 'I'm going to have to manage on my own.' But I was always thinking about the team, about all of us. I knew how to do that. I had been isolated at Chelsea for a season and a half, so if I'm given the ball, I'm going to make sure and return the favour. If I had the feeling it was a one-way relationship, I didn't act the same way back. I wanted to change the philosophy.

After that, I think he understood that I wasn't there to hurt him or the team. There were no stars in our group, only players committed to Mourinho's message. The team and winning were our priorities. Our strength lay in individuals' ability to work for the team.

Furthermore, I've already achieved all of the individual goal and match records I'm interested in. Like at Marseille. With more than 60 matches and 33 goals in all competitions I became the highest scorer in the English league, but we didn't win the title. That made it a team failure.

The team had lost its toughness, its willingness to play ugly football if necessary to win games. The season before that we were tearing ourselves apart or counting on an extremely strong defence. We had scraped a few 1–0s, enough to get the three points and the title. William Gallas's leaving the side did a lot to weaken our performance. I said so behind closed doors.

Somewhere along the way, the problems Ballack and Shevchenko, our two star signings, were having in adapting had cost us points and the title. These difficulties had indirectly upset our game. Nevertheless, we'd put in some really beautiful performances, especially in the Champions League, but we'd gone off the boil in the League.

Mourinho tried to give us a boost. I think he was perhaps the only one who still believed in destiny. He was convinced that Man U would trip up, and he was right, but we didn't take advantage of it. That irritated him until the very end; seeing us miss chances in matches, lack consistency. I can still hear him saying 'You don't want to be champions, but we're going to be!' over and over again. Maybe if there had been eleven Mourinhos on the pitch . . .

Still, we had a great run in the Champions League. We were missing key players at important moments. When everyone was available, the manager had choices, multiple options. Furthermore, he may not have received the support he was hoping for. He wanted to sign new players, particularly a centre back in December because of injuries. The management didn't agree.

Mourinho felt that control over signings was being taken away from him, that his position was starting to get fragile. It was becoming harder for him to keep control. I believe the decision to bench Sheva had muddied his relationship with the chairman somewhat. I don't think Roman Abramovich understood how the Ukrainian could perform so well at AC Milan and fail to do so in the Premier League. Was it because of the system the Portuguese coach had put in place?

*

Still, we won the F.A. Cup (1–0. a.e.t.) against Manchester United, our successors in the League, thanks to one of my goals. At the end of the match, I ran to the dressing room to speak to Mourinho. Many people saw it as a goodbye gesture, proof that the manager would be leaving the club at the end of the season. We had been hearing rumours of a possible split, of more and more obvious tensions. There was nothing really very spectacular about my gesture, and nothing exceptional in Mourinho's. He likes to call his wife after the games, so he had taken refuge inside the stadium, far from all the noise. That was just part of his personality.

Personally, I just wanted to speak to him, not because of our collaboration in general terms, but because of a specific piece of advice he had given me at a key moment in the final. I felt drained during extra time and I couldn't keep going forward. I was right on the edge. He spoke to me on the touch line: 'Come on, keep it up, you're going to score. It'll come. Stay focused.' The look on his face, the strength of his words told me he was convinced.

And four minutes from the end I did score. I didn't even have enough strength left to celebrate the goal with a victory lap or a dance. I was done. Mourinho's ability to see into the future again. That encouragement made the difference. I wanted to thank him for those words, something I've always been grateful for, and for that happy outcome.

Inevitably, in a season where you lose the League, tensions start to appear. When new players come in and results don't follow, people tend to imagine that things were better before. People don't take a step back and look at their own performances before blaming the newcomers. Our mistake was this short-sighted analysis: it was like claiming our record was enough, as if being champions would win us the title again, like showing up was enough to win.

We didn't try our hardest. It was the senior players' fault, and I include myself in that. Still, the newcomers could have contributed more to the team in terms of experience, especially against Liverpool in the Champions League semi-final. We didn't get the support we had been expecting. At some point along the way, those feelings turned the atmosphere more negative. Not hostile, though. There was no animosity among us. When things weren't going well in the League, we forgot to look ourselves in the mirror. We blamed colleagues instead. It's no exaggeration to say it was a year filled with regrets. We also saw that our two successive titles had created jealousy, that an anti-Chelsea storm was blowing up.

How can we accept what happened at Reading in October? Our two goalkeepers, Petr Cech then Carlo Cudicini, had to leave the pitch after violent clashes. We were really worried about Petr, who suffered a cranial fracture. He had been kneed in the temple by Hunt in the opening minute. Petr was inches from dying. If it hadn't been for quick surgery, he might not be with us today. I was worried stiff for days and days. When we visited Petr in hospital it was very tense. We didn't know if he'd ever play again . . .

When playing, we often felt our opponents wanted to get stuck in to Chelsea. I'm not being paranoid, they would come after us. It's natural to want to beat the champions, but you can't do it at all costs.

Personally, I was in great shape. I rattled matches off. I was feeling less tired, even if fatigue would catch up with me in the end.

In those really busy moments, the doping question inevitably gets brought up, especially in France. When you look at the English Premiership, it's hard to imagine having so many top-level matches one after the other without needing to use illegal substances. Perhaps I would think the same thing if I'd never come to England. Here, if you lose your form you can quickly lose your place. Obviously, there is therapeutic follow-up, like at all clubs, like at Marseille. I have too much respect for my body and what will happen after my career to get involved in doping.

It's a question of will, of your personal goals. I judged myself by one standard: can I do better than at Marseille? Some days I didn't play well, but I scored. I ran less and I paced myself better. I used my experience, my knowledge of the game, of my opponents. In the end, I became better than I was at Marseille.

That's how I came into rivalry with the Manchester United forward Cristiano Ronaldo for best player in England. An added bonus of which I was proud. He and I had similar stories. When he first arrived in England, he was met by quite a few jeers. He was roasted in the media after the 2006 World Cup.* An unfair campaign was waged against him. He was destroyed by the supporters. I encountered similar treatment two months earlier. That brought us closer. Quite by accident, we found ourselves in close competition and our fight was a long one. What riled me was that each time I scored, he would score too! He kept upping his performances. I don't know how many points Ronaldo won for Manchester United. He broke through a ceiling that season, and his consistency had a great influence on Man Utd's game. He had finally fully adapted, just as I had.

We have very different styles: he leaves men for dead, he strikes, he's spectacular. His acceleration is phenomenal. Personally, my game is more based on my movement, my scoring instinct, my feeling for the pitch. But we're both strong-minded. We never give anything away, even in the most difficult moments. I finished the second-best player in the league, just behind him, but I still felt good.

By the end of the season no one was slagging me off any more. Over the year, even our supporters at Chelsea had taken up chants the Marseille fans used to use. It happened on the afternoon of our second title win. I was taking a lap of honour with the trophy when suddenly I heard 'Didier Drogbalalalalala' echoing down from the stands. I stopped in my tracks . . . I

---

* He pointed the finger at Rooney, his teammate at Manchester United, for stepping on Ricardo Carvalho in the quarter-finals of Euro 2006. That got the English player sent off.

had to be imagining it. Marseille fans at Stamford Bridge? Was it a joke? No. Chelsea fans then joined in with a chorus of chanting. That was the end of the old song based on my name that ended 'boubou'. I always hated that song. A kind of belch. I felt like I was back at Marseille all of a sudden, and I revelled in it, though without the sound of the gulls. Feelings came flooding back. That song would accompany my goals. I owed it to myself to have a season like at Marseille. But did it stop me wanting to leave? If I'm honest, the answer is no.

I had won everything I could in London, except the Champions League. I thought it was time to pack my bags again. I think that third season enabled me to win people's respect. That was so important to me. Leaving on a high note would mean a lot. I thought the manager was going to leave too, but he stayed. I was trying to see what my options were. I love challenges, having to prove myself again. What would I be capable of achieving in the Italian or Spanish leagues? I wanted to take the risk and find out. I'm not scared of failing – it's never killed anyone after all. But I couldn't do it. Could I really throw away my relationship with José Mourinho? I didn't think so. In the life of a football player, you run into some people and they change you for ever.

12

MR JOSÉ MOURINHO

Our first meeting had been strange. It was in the corridor of the Vélodrome Stadium at half-time in the Marseille–Porto match during the group stages of the Champions League. José Mourinho shouted a few nice words at me and flashed a charming smile. 'So tell me, where can I get a player like you? Do you have a brother or a cousin in the Ivory Coast? Because I don't have the money to buy you for Porto.' I replied that the attention was very kind. I was impressed by his command of French and his charm. It was the beginning of a beautiful story. When he later left Porto for Chelsea, signing me became his priority. He swore to me that he had often watched my progress at OM. He was impressed by the performances I'd put in, the way I carried myself on the pitch, the reputation I had earned from my efforts.

José knew exactly what role he wanted me to have in his team. He simply looked me in the eye and said: 'I trust you.' Without any pretence. Mourinho isn't a coach who trains players, he takes on people who are ready to adhere to his philosophy. What's more, they're not necessarily the best players in the world. I will never forget what he said when we met in Paris just as everything was being decided. I had to leave Marseille. I explained my position to him, the passion I felt for the club, my doubts and worries. His response was: 'You're a very good player. I know what you mean to the fans at Marseille because I played against the team with Porto. But now, if you want to become one of the greats, like Henry, Ronaldo, van Nistelrooy, you have to come and play for me!' When a manager of his class says something like that, it's hard to remain indifferent. He wanted to move me into Europe's big league. That first approach sums up our working relationship, based on mutual respect. If it weren't for him, I'm sure I wouldn't have stayed at Chelsea, or even come in the first place. If it weren't for him, I might not have filled my trophy cabinet as quickly.

He was my rock in hard times, the manager who always stood up for me against the critics. His words reassured me a great deal. At the beginning of my second season, he answered those who thought I hadn't scored enough by saying, 'It doesn't matter if Didier scores or not as long as Chelsea wins. People don't realise just how fundamentally important he is to the team, even when he doesn't score. He's a great player because he has fantastic spirit and puts the team first. He fights for Chelsea, not for statistics.' Then later, 'The team wouldn't be the same without Drogba,' and 'If I had to go into battle and I could choose a player to go with me, there's only one I'd want: Didier. Because he's a fantastic guy.' In his last full year, he said, 'I have three irreplaceable players: Ricardo Carvalho, John Terry and Didier Drogba.' How can you not feel that you owe something to someone like that?

He was always praising me. He picked me so he always defended me. When you think that Mourinho had favoured an unknown player from the Ivory Coast over Ronaldo or Shevchenko, two of the top forwards in the world, it says more for what he thinks about me than a whole mouthful of words. I could only thank him for that trust.

I liked the way he protected us. Helped us. His inaugural season-opening speech touched me right away. 'The title is between Manchester United, Arsenal and us. We will only be champions if we beat weaker teams. Then we have to beat one of the big teams or draw. It's not important. But we must never lose against the small teams. If we win away or at home, we'll be champions.' Know how to concentrate on what are easy opponents on paper; never underestimate an opponent. That was his theory.

At one point in the first season we were a little adrift of Arsenal, but that didn't worry him. 'You'll see, we'll catch up. Arsenal will drop points here and there.' That's exactly what happened. He had a gift for predicting things. He could foresee what the result of a match would be. I heard him describe what would happen from the bench, almost down to the last detail. It was amazing. Sometimes, that vision which was so close to reality could be worrying. As if he could see the future. It was really strange.

At Chelsea, he was smart enough to accept the club's background and customs rather than imposing his own. He never said, 'Well, I'm Mourinho and I don't want to see that any more. I don't care about your traditions!' No, he arrived at the club and he adapted. In particular, he kept the music and TV in the dressing room. Afterwards, on the pitch, he brought his know-how, his ability to please.

His professionalism was extreme. Before each match, we each had two or three pages to read. Everything was written down, the make-up of the opposing team, his tactical diagram away from home, at home. Every last detail. The key points were highlighted in red. We had a profile of our opponents, their favourite moves, notes on our opposite number: was he risking a suspension if carded, did he like to go left or right . . . This almost scientific approach pushed us to seeing football from a different angle. More professional, more modern. We felt we knew more than our opponents did. That's how we approached Scunthorpe United, a Fourth Division team, in the Cup (3–1): extremely thorough tactical work using video. We knew the essential information, right up to the way their penalty specialist liked to kick.

And it didn't stop there. He calculated everything. He would look at the calendar, analyse each of his boys' cards.

Sometimes he'd just say: 'It would be good for you to get a yellow card today. You'll miss such and such a match. I'll give you four days off.' No problem. I did my stuff and it gave me the chance to do a quick round trip to Dubai. He customised the strategy for each player.

He had infected us with the victory virus, the desire to always win. Only success mattered. His provocations were almost like entertainment to him. The pressure placed on him didn't weigh upon his players. He also believed that the more time opposing managers spent getting angry, the less time they had to dissect his game. Shrewd of him.

We appreciated each other. He would often come to see me before I was 100 per cent recovered from an injury: 'How are you feeling Didier?'

'Sixty per cent. But coach, I'm going to give 100 per cent of my 60 per cent.' He'd laugh. It became an in-joke between us. We were often seen as a team in the press. One day, a newspaper headline about him read: 'He's going to leave' or 'He has to go'. The photo they picked had him beside me, as a coincidence . . .

Our close relationship didn't stop us from having quite a quarrel, which influenced my third season at Chelsea. It was a decisive part of my year, the highlight of which was when I was named top scorer in the League.

As we came to the end of the transfer window, on 23 August 2006 we were defeated by Middlesbrough (2–1). It was a physically trying match. I got knocks everywhere. I wasn't really at my peak yet for the new season, so I was more sensitive than normal. My body wasn't ready to take all the hits, and my mind was elsewhere. William Gallas had just left the club. Allowing Gallas to go to Arsenal had really made me angry . . . He and Terry formed the best pair of central defenders in the world in my opinion. When Ricardo Carvalho was added to the mix, there was no one else like those three. That was huge and very reassuring. Gallas hadn't received the respect he deserved. At some point, a misunderstanding came between the two sides and it was never sorted out.

Without William we lost at Boro. The referee didn't step in to help me out and I was treated harshly. Four days later, at Blackburn, I was on the bench. That rejection annoyed me. I didn't say anything, but I wasn't speaking to the coach. It was the first time he'd overlooked me without so much as an explanation.

This decision came after an incident in the dressing room during the game against Liverpool in the Community Shield, the opening game of the season. Mourinho said, 'Don't give the ball to Didier, he's having trouble keeping it. Pass it through Shevchenko instead, he's better technically.' Then, speaking to Sheva, who'd scored already, 'Don't run so much, don't defend so much! Stay in your outside position.' I couldn't believe my ears. Had I heard him right? I looked at the coach and wondered, 'Is he serious, or is he having me on? What's going on?' Worst of all, he wasn't laughing. He was entirely serious. We lost to Liverpool (2–1).

Questions were still running through my mind as I sat on the bench at Blackburn. I felt he was doing everything he could to favour Sheva. Negative images wormed their way into my head.

The staff sent me to warm up during the second half of the Blackburn match. When I stepped up to go on the pitch, Steve Clarke, Mourinho's deputy, said to me, 'Show him you deserve to play. That you shouldn't have been benched today!' Steve understood that I was disappointed. People at the club learned to read my thoughts and I'm not the sort of guy who can easily hide his emotions. He knew I was angry with the coach, and also that I could contribute in that match. I came on, Essien fed me the ball just beating the offside trap, and I snatched a goal.

I was so angry that I pushed away Shevchenko, who was first to come and congratulate me. I would have reacted the same with anyone. I didn't jump for joy. The fact I'd been sat on the bench was sticking in my throat.

After that, Mourinho gave us two rest days as we had to join up with our national teams. I was going to Nice where Ivory Coast was playing a friendly against the local team.

Two days earlier I had asked Mourinho for permission to travel to Paris to see my dentist. He said yes. So I rented a private jet from Manchester to Paris.

But meanwhile my dentist had cancelled our appointment, so I decided to go to Milan instead and have a good time as it isn't far from Nice. I flew out with Cudicini, our goalkeeper, and I left him at his home. Then I went to eat with some friends, Paolo Maldini and Christian Vieri, in an Italian restaurant. Just as I was arriving, I ran into Adriano Galliani, the deputy chairman of AC Milan, as he was coming out of the same smart restaurant. It was the end of August. We struck up a conversation.

– When are you coming to play for Milan?

– Whenever you want. It's up to you. Just put up the cash and go speak to Chelsea.

– You know we tried to get you when we sold them Sheva, but they weren't interested.

– Try again.

We more or less ended our conversation with those words. That evening, news of our meeting was on *Sky Sport Italy*. 'Galliani runs into Drogba in Milan with Maldini.' That was all it took for some people to see my leaving Chelsea as behind my visit to Milan. When, really, I was there to have a good time. I think Galliani called Peter Kenyon the next day and made an offer. Maldini may also have supported that request . . . You see, during our meal I had explained to him that Milan was a club I'd like to go to; that if I left Chelsea, it would be to go to that legendary European club. All footballers dream of AC Milan. Maldini explained to me that they needed forwards. Oliveira and Ronaldo hadn't arrived yet. Maldini said I had the goal-scoring profile they needed. We laughed about it at the table. 'Can you see me in a Milan strip?' It made me think.

The Lombardy club offered 30 million euros for me. I honestly thought it would happen. I sincerely believe that those in charge considered accepting that offer at one point. Thirty million for a 28-year-old bought for 37: the club had got its money's worth, hadn't lost anything. I'd won two titles, two Cups and there comes a time when things just seem logical. Chelsea was ready. They sounded out my agent, Thierno.

After my break in Milan, I joined up with the Ivory Coast team in Nice. I received voice-mail messages from Gary Stecker, Chelsea's bursar, who is in permanent contact with the manager. The first said: 'Didier, it's Gary, call me when you get this message.' Then a second: 'We still haven't received the fax from the Ivory Coast Federation. If it doesn't come through you're going to have to come back very quickly.' The way he was speaking was completely out of character for such a sweet guy. Finally, a third: 'You have to come back.' Our friendly was set for the Friday. The Ivory Coast still didn't have a manager after Henri Michel's departure following the World Cup. That little hitch caused a few administrative details to be overlooked, but it didn't matter.

I called Stecker.

– Gary, what's up?

– We have four fax numbers here and we haven't received anything! The coach says you've got to come back.

– We're not children, so tell me what's really wrong.

All of a sudden, it was José on the other end of the phone. I'm sure that Peter Kenyon must have been there, that they put the phone on conference mode. Then the coach lost his temper:

– OK, as we're not kids, let's talk! I trusted you, I've done everything for you. You said you were going to Paris when in fact you were in Milan to talk about your transfer! You lied to me, your word is meaningless. You're like Makelele [at the time there was a problem concerning Claude and the French team]. Were you badly brought up, or something?

– Stop! Say whatever you want, but don't start on my upbringing!

– We haven't received the fax, so if we don't get it you're coming back, you're not on leave like the others and you'll train with the reserves.

– No problem. If there's no fax, I'll come back.

– Even if you do get one.

– No worries, I'll play the game against Nice and I'll be right back.

That's the way it happened. I trained with the reserves. I explained to him why I was in Milan. My meeting with Galliani was purely by chance. That was the first time I trained with the B team since my arrival at Chelsea. The next day, he put me in the line-up with the reserves against West Ham. It was 0–0 at half-time when he arrived. I was taken off when we were losing (1–0). Essien was also in that team. We went on to win after I was substituted! It was a bit embarrassing . . .

In any case, things were clear for me. I could say to myself that there were teams looking to buy me. My value was recognised and it touched me. Even in England, certain clubs recognised my class, respected me. For about two weeks, José and I would see one another but we avoided each other like kids. Like a father and son who weren't speaking. And then we had a match against Liverpool. I scored just before half-time.

The TV showed José getting up, but not coming towards me. He left. That was his thank you. Suddenly, I felt like going towards the bench to celebrate, before getting a grip on myself and going to the other side of the pitch! It wasn't yet time to really make up. But it would soon come . . .

He would always give us the plan for the entire month, which players were resting or training and when. I was busy noting down my days off on my mobile. We were in the club's physio room at Cobham. José saw me – he looked pretty excited, and laughed: 'So Didier, you're preparing for Milan already.' I looked at him and didn't answer. Then I said seriously, 'Next time I'm in Milan, I'll actually sign an agreement!' We looked at each other and burst out laughing. The squabble was over. The only time we'd had a misunderstanding was just swept away.

I'd wanted to leave Chelsea at some point each season, but I don't think I could have with José there. Something brought us close, connected us, like a secret pact. Looks, feelings. He brought me to Chelsea, helped me renegotiate my pay in my third season – an important time for me. I gave him a lot, but he gave a lot back.

I took his departure as a huge slap in the face. With him I played 140 matches and scored 70 goals in a Chelsea strip. He was a man you couldn't possibly ignore. Maybe our paths will cross again some day. Actually, I'm sure of it. He swore to me he'd like to work with me again and given his gift for predicting the future, he must have a precise date in mind . . .

13

LEAVING

The club punched me in the face. To be fair, I should have seen it coming. José Mourinho had been out on a limb for a long time; he was only hanging on thanks to magical, unbeatable results. Chelsea had learned to win, with the happiness that brought, and had taken its place on the national and European stage.

How else could I have reacted? My professional life would be dull without Mourinho. He had welcomed me to Chelsea with open arms. I couldn't just look the other way when he left. I found out about it almost by chance the day before the announcement. We ran into each other at the club, just after he'd been told by the directors themselves.

I'm a flesh-and-blood human being. I was touched, and

terribly sorry. The path we shared had come to an end too soon, with a feeling of unfinished business. There was nothing we could do. There are some scenes in dressing rooms that can't help but move you. He came to Cobham, the training centre, the next day. It was like being struck.

He told us, in a few simple words and gestures, he had been let go. We saw him holding back his sadness. He left as he had arrived: strong, self-confident. It was quick – five minutes and that was it. He finished by embracing all the players. Well, almost . . . 'I wish you all and all your families good luck and I thank you. Even those of you who betrayed me!'

We knew it was coming, but we didn't understand why. I couldn't help shedding tears when I hugged him goodbye. It was all too much. He had cleared his desk very quickly. Just bizarre. It was very moving.

There were also several people on his staff who we were close to. So it affected all of us. It was hard to look certain people in the eye without wanting to flare up. Still, Mourinho let his guard down for a second: 'I want you to know that I'm very happy to be leaving here.' What did he mean? I was scared of going off on one – some of my reactions then didn't seem appropriate or professional.

I felt like an orphan. Of course, there were the pro-Mourinhos among us, of which I was one, and then there were the others. That's how it goes at the top. His leaving suited some team members – they were getting a new chance, a new beginning perhaps. Hope sprang anew for some people. I wasn't going to be preaching to anyone. We're all fathers at

Chelsea. I'd already lived through this sort of thing at Marseille when Alain Perrin left. We can understand it but we don't have to like it. I was saddened because I liked working with him.

I wasn't the only one. You could see dejection on some people's faces. There's no need for words at times like that. Starting to train again was awful. I was just getting over an injury and was in the middle of physiotherapy. I have the scene etched on my mind: I was with a club physio the day after the boss's departure. Brito, one of his deputies, came to say goodbye to us because he hadn't been there the night before. He was a member of the staff, those loyal people who acted as sounding boards when we needed to speak to someone without going to José.

I was no good out there on the training pitch. We talked a little. I couldn't use my legs, they just wouldn't carry me. I wasn't able to work for three or four days. I waited for it to pass, then tried to get back into the swing. That's one of the hardest things at times like that. You start chewing everything over, especially the idea of leaving. You start thinking about your future and whether it lies elsewhere.

I was also upset for my friend Florent Malouda, because I had pushed to get him to the club. Like a child showing off his toys, I'd wanted him to discover Mourinho's methods, which were partly what brought him here. I was sad that he would get the wrong image of Chelsea, sad to see the manager who'd been so keen to sign him discarded so soon.

But I had to get back down to work. It was as simple as that.

I took my time getting better. I was concerned about being stupid and coming back too quickly, of injuring myself through thinking too much about the team and not enough about my health. My first game back was against Fulham in the League. I was very nervous and ended up getting sent off. I picked up my first yellow card for back-chat, and the second for a very clumsy move. I raised my knee up to my opponent's chest. It was a fair sending-off, but it was a shame, I'd never had a red card in the Premier League.

And it all added to my foul mood. I'd had it up to here. Next was a group-stages game against Valencia in the Champions League. I was asking myself question after question after question. In my head I wanted to be gone. Should I try to get out during the winter transfer window or wait till the end of the season? If I left in January it would be for a club that had the Continent's big prize in its sights.

In that case, I shouldn't take part in the Champions League with Chelsea, because you can't play in the Champions League for two clubs in the same season. It was a terrible bind. I was ready to stay out of it now so I could take part with a different club later on. I was feeling headstrong, still thinking in the heat of the moment – listening to my heart, not my head. That's not always the best way to make important decisions. I wavered right up to the night before our shock in Spain. Should I do it or not? Go or stay? My agent Thierno set things straight. I spoke with Pape Diouf, the Marseille chairman and my ex-agent. We talked it over and he managed to calm me down a bit.

As always, he found the right words to get me back on the right track. In those moments when your future is on the line, it's important to have people you trust around you, people with your interests at heart, not their own. If I had gone through with it, it would have been hard to look my colleagues in the face.

I scored the next day and helped set up the second. People who watched the match said I put in a really good performance. But I didn't feel involved, I was there without actually being there. The passion, the rivalry, never took hold. I'm a little off-beat at times, but it's the way I see things: it's hard to change something like that. As I've said before, it's never been about the money for me. What counts is the relationships I've struck up over the years. Once again I needed to get things off my chest, to have my say. I decided to do an interview with Pascal Ferré, a journalist friend of mine from *France Football*, in Austria where I was with the Ivory Coast team. We discussed Chelsea. I wanted people to understand me. I admit I made a mistake, I should have talked it over with the management first, kept my feelings inside the club. But every last word I said had been weighed up and thought through. I wanted to leave. Was this a surprise?

Everyone thought my feelings were to do with Mourinho leaving. That was partly true, but not 100 per cent. The idea had been in my head for so long. His sacking was just another reason. Not the only reason though. Quite simply, the moment had come. It's true that all of this happened in a single season. You have to be able to deal with that, to be up to the challenge, ready to perform.

I'm not sure if I was lucky, but by venting my anger, I grieved losing Mourinho. I needed to open up. It was a way of saying: 'I don't care any more, I'm going to play and have a good time.' While keeping to my group philosophy, Chelsea's central guideline, and respecting the fans, the new coach, the management and my teammates. I didn't want anyone to come up with digs like 'You say one thing and do another.' No, I wanted to be consistent, I always do what I say I'm going to do.

At Chelsea, however, it was action stations. *France Football* hit the newsstands on Friday, but snippets were already available on Thursday as soon as the magazine was printed. When the management got wind of the extracts, they called my agents: 'What's going on?' My agents didn't really know . . . They should have phoned me instead.

Before leaving for Middlesbrough on the Friday I saw Peter Kenyon.

– What was that interview about?

– I gave them an article.

– Do you want us to issue a denial?

– No, it was perfect. It's exactly what I said. I want to leave.

– Yes, but you talked about stuff that happened in the dressing room.

– Tell me one bad thing I said about another player in that interview. I said I wanted to leave and I don't see what's wrong with that. If a player feels he was targeted, that's his problem.

To cool things down, the club issued a press release on their website: Drogba has signed a contract tying him to the club until 2010.

That incident stands out as a unique moment in my life in London. I hoped I was in my last year at Chelsea. I didn't know what the future held for me, but I let it be known I wished to leave because I wanted to start again from scratch, try something new. But I have never forgotten what Chelsea has given me in terms of recognition. I would like to thank the club and its fans: they pushed me to the forefront of the international stage.

Getting back on top form after my statements was essential. The supporters could have turned on me, insulted me, called me a coward, a traitor, shouted at me that I was disrespecting the club. But that didn't happen. I notched up some important goals after all of this. Like at Middlesbrough, where I kissed the Chelsea badge after I scored. That gesture was for the fans. I didn't kiss the jersey, I kissed the supporters. I like the way they admitted their mistake about me. They managed to say: 'We were the first to start criticising when you arrived, but now you're number one.' I respect that. My first match at Stamford Bridge after this episode, against the German team Schalke in the Champions League, was fabulous: the fans chanted my name. I was proud to be at Chelsea, proud of what I'd achieved since arriving. I'm not saying this to soften what I said. I've been pretty true to my feelings in this book, even if that bothers some people. I never meant to mess anybody up.

During my time in London, I finally learned to love the people who follow us. I shocked them sometimes, I amazed them with my statements. But I've never abandoned them on the pitch. I've never given anything but 100 per cent, for them and for myself; for Chelsea and for myself. I believe that deep down, they discovered who I was, learned to feel my reactions, read my thoughts; to understand that beneath my shell, what may seem like my arrogance, I'm a sensitive sort of guy. They were wary when I first arrived at Chelsea, they sometimes booed me. But they took me in as one of their own. As a true Blue.

14

ELEPHANT HEART

The call from Côte d'Ivoire took me by surprise. I had just started the season at Guingamp and shown a glimpse of my potential against Lyon, the French title-holders.

In fact I was lucky, in that Robert Nouzaret was the selector of the Elephants. He'd known me for some time – I had impressed him by scoring for Le Mans in the French Cup against Bastia, the Ligue 1 club he managed. He hadn't forgotten me, and had even sent a scout to follow my career, aiming to sign me eventually. What a stroke of luck – he had left Corsica for Côte d'Ivoire!

So there I was with my future teammates near Roissy Charles de Gaulle airport in August 2002, in a huge room at the hotel where we were staying. It was a simple get-together organised by Nouzaret and Jacques Anouma, the new president of our federation, without a match coming up. It was basically a chance to get to know each other, find out what our fellow teammates were like. Anouma had decided to draw a line under the errors of the past and impose some guidelines on the team. There'd be no more letting things slide, no more time-wasting. A new spirit was to emerge from this meeting. The president explained what he expected from us, his ambition and hope to see us in Germany for the 2006 World Cup. The 2004 African Cup of Nations in Tunisia was clearly an aim, but not the final aim. He wanted to take the world by storm, put the Elephants on the map. The World Cup! The Elephants had never flown so high.

I sat in my corner and listened. Around the table were players like Cyril Domoraud of Inter Milan and Marseille, Bonaventure Kalou who'd just won the UEFA Cup with Feyenoord, and many others with far more claims to fame than my own. I watched them, wide-eyed – they were icons to me, as I was just starting out in Ligue 1.

At first the president's goal seemed unreal, beyond our reach. We'd finished the last two African Cup of Nations tournaments with crushing defeats, two first-round knock-outs. We needed to return to the muscular form of the 2000 squad, which spent several days in a military camp after its failure, during the time of General Gueï, a reining-in that concerned more than a few people.

As a Franco-Ivorian, I could have chosen to play for Les Bleus, but I had never been selected in the youth squads – which given my unusual career path was no surprise.

So there was no real choice for me. Jacques Santini, then the French selector, looked into my case a few days later, but it was already too late – I had chosen my side. My first impressions were good – my heart pulled me to my home country. On 21 August we played a friendly against Créteil, and I scored my first goal for the team. I was a true Elephant, facing a speciality of our country – endless and fruitless meetings! I soon realised this was an incurable illness. Anyone who's never discussed bonuses would have trouble imagining just how long the negotiations can drag on. On the positive side, they allow things to be said face to face, which is no bad thing. These endless meetings are like group therapy without a doctor or a shrink. These crucial matters, these sensitive and never-ending discussions where you have to be so careful not to hurt anyone's feelings, have often led to disagreements between the federations and the players.

At those times, only senior players like Bakayoko, Domoraud and Lassina Diabaté, a French champion with Bordeaux, were allowed to speak. I felt at home right from the start in my orange shirt, although also a little intimidated. I could feel that Nouzaret trusted me and that I fitted into his plans. In my first official match I played against South Africa in Abidjan. How could I ever forget this amazing moment? Me, the minnow, at the Félix Houphouët-Boigny stadium . . . In the temple of Ivorian football. Just imagine – I'd never played in Africa, never set foot on this scrubby grass, this rough ground.

In the week leading up to this event I had to deal with my first-ever scandal. With our captain Tchiressoua Guel gone, the question of his successor poisoned our first days in training. All this was new to me. There was a vote to determine who would get to wear the armband. Five or six players were shortlisted. Naturally I wasn't one of them. But I appreciated how Serge Dié, Cyril Domoraud, Blaise Kouassi and Jean-Jacques Tizié, the goalkeeper, treated me, letting me in on their meetings. It was the best way for a young player like me to understand the flipside of the coin in an African selection, to see how problems with captaincy and money were handled . . . It was clever of them.

They ended up picking Domoraud, which didn't please Ibrahim Bakayoko, who confronted the bosses. Robert Nouzaret, a trainer not known for messing about, didn't hesitate: he sent him home. The decision came as a bombshell. At home it caused absolute mayhem. They were doing away with the best striker for the African Cup of Nations qualifiers, which meant I was suddenly propelled to the front line, leading the attack with Bonaventure Kalou by my side. It was a huge responsibility for my baptism in official competition. And in my own country.

Some encounters mark you for life. Years later you can still picture every moment, every colour, breathe in every smell. That Ivory Coast–South Africa meeting was one of them.

The heat was stifling, suffocating. Recalling that Sunday afternoon of 8 September 2002 is like walking into a sauna. The thermometer read over 40 degrees in the shade. The stadium sits in a basin – there's no wind, no shade where you could hide from sunstroke. And the weather was just so close . . . Welcome to Abidjan. It was really hot and I had to find ways to cool off. My shoes were burning and I was drinking non-stop. I tried pouring water in my shoes, but within seconds it would be scalding hot again! My poor feet were in agony.

So we had to save our energy. Every sprint drained my strength, stole my breath. The only person who seemed to be on fire and going for it was Kanga Akalé. He was always on the move, dribbling, passing. Without question he played the best of all of us. I didn't get to score, despite two or three chances, but it didn't matter. They held us to a draw (0–0). For the first time in my life, I'd got goose bumps as I walked onto the pitch, greeting the crowd who'd come to welcome us. And the anthem! Such strong feelings. As I watched those people who'd come to support us, the hairs on my body stood on end. The whole stadium sang and shouted. It was an extraordinary experience. I felt so proud to see my country again, to represent it, to wear this orange skin. On the plane back that evening my toes were so swollen that I couldn't put my shoes back on. It felt like pain and magic combined – I was in absolute agony but all I wanted was to do it all over again as soon as possible.

*

Sadly, ten days later the Côte d'Ivoire was plunged into chaos, into civil war. During the night of 18 September 2002 the country was suddenly bathed in a mist of tears, cut in half with the north held by the rebels and the south by the government.

With time, we would come to represent a kind of national hope, a symbol for unity and peace. I spoke about this at the beginning of this book and I will talk about it again at length. We have never wanted to stray from that path.

The friendly match against Cameroon in Châteauroux (3–0) in February 2003 convinced us of our potential. The Lions Indomptables (Indomitable Lions) were strutting around as two-time African champions, which had forced us to take things seriously, to play a more complete game. In the changing rooms the lead singer of Magic System hummed 'Premier Gaou', the hit of the moment in Abidjan and Paris. He sung our praises. People believed in our team. Here in this damp room, we had a crazy feeling, an omen of the years to come. A terrific atmosphere.

Unfortunately, that draw with South Africa had almost knocked us out of the 2004 ACN. In our group of three, we'd failed to reverse the trend by losing, away from home, a match we could have won (2–1). This was bad luck. For the first time Côte d'Ivoire wouldn't be making it to the final stage of the African Cup of Nations. We weren't well enough prepared, but we'd shown potential.

In retrospect, I was certain that this team could actually have won the ACN in Tunisia thanks to its balance of youth and experience.

Jacques Anouma never went against his principles – he wanted the World Cup and wasn't prepared to make wholesale changes the way so many African countries are used to doing. He took the long view, refusing to be fazed by a temporary setback. Robert Nouzaret however quit for personal reasons and Henri Michel, with his incomparable record, took over as trainer. The president of the federation was looking for an experienced coach. We talked it over and looked for leads. Michel stood out. He spoke our language and Anouma wanted a man with World Cup experience. With three World Cups on his CV (with France, Cameroon and Morocco), Michel was the perfect choice, someone capable of taking Côte d'Ivoire to Germany. He was the right man, as will become clear later on.

Of course, we would achieve this milestone in Ivory Coast football only after unimaginable suspense and desperate efforts, at the end of the qualifying stage. But our goal would be attained, and that's what mattered. Does any team find it easy to qualify for a World Cup, an African or European Cup? Didn't England go through this bitter experience when Croatia kicked it out of the 2008 European Championships? And in our group, Cameroon and Egypt were forces to be reckoned with.

Henri had his own old-school style. He had an aloof side, kept a certain distance from physical exercise and matches. People would get grouchy during training sessions but his work bore its fruits. We worked in groups and that created bonds and solidarity. I was the one who'd ended up with the armband and I'd been accepted as a leader. I hadn't decreed or requested anything – the others had handed me this power. I'd always wanted to get involved in the selection process, to give it a little more discipline, of the kind I'd learned with the European clubs. My views carried weight. I'd pushed Dagui Bakari to put on the national shirt, and I wasn't afraid to tell a few home truths. After one clash, I started to talk. 'It's important to talk about things; we're not here to mouth platitudes. There may be mornings when we can't bring ourselves to say hi, but it doesn't matter because this is a collective project and the reward is the same for everyone.' I'd also give out a few tactical pointers, I'd get stuck in.

As the months went by, I discovered a new world. Our bus would echo with the sound of song, and people would dance in the aisles, everyone doing their thing. Life, basically – the good mood was contagious. I myself was used to the European way of getting ready and I felt completely out of sync, culturally. In France we weren't allowed to use mobile phones, and prepping for an event was no laughing matter; in Africa on the other hand, there was this constant bustle, excitement and noise, laughter and slaps on the back. How does that stop anyone from playing well?

Henri Michel accepted all this commotion without blinking – he enjoyed the vibe, just like Robert Nouzaret, another follower of these methods. It didn't stop us from getting good results – on the contrary, it was a natural way to release stress.

What's more, we were like a ray of sunshine in a country plunged into grave crisis. We had to keep going. The elephant would stampede prejudice, crush it out. Whenever we heard about the country being set ablaze for ethnic reasons, we'd display our differences as so many reasons to stay positive and avoid jumping to conclusions or getting too pessimistic.

But all together, we did experience the darkest hour of our career with the Elephants, the day where Mama Ouattara, Henri Michel's assistant, died. This was the first time in my life I'd been faced with death – I'd never seen it up close, been touched by it so directly. We were training at Moissy-Cramayel before travelling to Egypt to play a World Cup elimination match. We'd just started a three-team tournament amongst ourselves and Mama got hit in the side with the ball. He carried on as normal and then suddenly collapsed, as though in slow motion. He fell to his knees and started choking; he began to swallow his tongue – it was horrible. We called the doctor. Just recalling this brings back horrific images . . . The paramedics arrived, and we just stood there, helpless, in the middle of the pitch.

For two or three hours we just wept, almost motionless on this bloody lawn. Lost in our pain, unable to grasp what had happened. It was so hard, so brutal.

Mama is someone I valued immensely. I'll never forget that night in January 2004 in Tunis when I'd got the best African player award alongside Samuel Eto'o from Cameroon.

Marseille had let me go to Tunisia just to collect the award –
this was quite an event in my burgeoning career. Mama came
with his wife to be a part of it, to congratulate me and to be
with me. 'We're here to support you,' he whispered to me in
that gentle voice of his. He had this cheerful, conspiratorial
way of looking at you and he was so pleased to see a son of our
country getting such a great accolade.

I was sincerely flattered that he'd even thought about me.
We took a few pictures, chatted for a few minutes – I can still
picture the scene at that hotel, near the buffet . . . Him and
her, then me, feeling a little intimidated in this world I was
only beginning to discover. I'd never experienced the African
Cup of Nations and the place was full of big names. I was
seated near Samuel Eto'o, who was already terrorising the
defenders of the Spanish championship.

Mama, who used to play for Montpellier, was still in top
physical shape at over 50 years of age. He was always up for a
training session or going for a jog. He was a strong guy, all
muscle.

Before his untimely death, we'd played a match against
Libya in Abidjan. I'd gone back to Paris and he'd stayed there.
We had two days off before meeting up near Paris, where we
would all gather.

We were glad to see each other at the hotel.

– How's it going Mama?

– I'm a bit tired; it was a long journey.

– You'd better rest because we're going to go for it this
afternoon!

He'd smiled – always so thoughtful and genuinely kind. We went off training and the warm-up was going well . . . I'll bear the scar of losing such a good friend for ever.

And to think that we still had a week of prepping left, with our training pitch right next to the place where this tragedy occurred . . . For two days we couldn't bring ourselves to go anywhere near it, it was too hard, too emotional, too brutal. We were staying in the same hotel and he had had his room there, right next door . . .

His family came down. How could I even begin to face such pain? His wife gave me the pictures we'd taken in Tunisia . . . It turned me inside out, I was overwhelmed. We were all affected. Mama had been the perfect complement to Henri Michel. He was close to the guys, he enjoyed listening to us. He had the soul of a coach, of a tutor and it was a great loss for all of us. Mama was a good man.

This event also opened my eyes; I realised that we were nothing but passengers on this planet. Four days after the tragedy, we were all sitting down for a meal. I was observing, still grieving, but life was asserting itself, people were laughing . . . Then I thought: 'Shit, is this all we are?' At that time I found this attitude shocking – I didn't understand, couldn't get over how bad I felt. The others were actually just as affected as I was, but they handled it in different ways; some just talked about it less than others.

This was the worst time in my Ivorian adventure. No joy can compensate for the loss of a life, the life of a friend . . .

*

After this tragedy, the World Cup became more than just a goal: it was an obligation. We made a kind of pact: we'd go to Germany for him. Mama had wanted us to so badly.

We beat Egypt (2–1) and I scored. I don't even know how I managed it; it was almost an impossible goal. Could it have been Mama's spirit? We dedicated this victory to him. Then we went to Cameroon with higher spirits but we lost (2–0) – we were exhausted, physically and mentally. That month spent together had brought tensions and disagreements. It was time to go home, before meeting Cameroon again later for revenge in Abidjan. We played in Montpellier, taking part in Zinédine Zidane's return to les Bleus. In light of the tensions between France and Côte d'Ivoire, that meeting in August 2005 couldn't have been better timed, from both a political and a sporting point of view. Zidane, Thuram and Makelele's returns to les Bleus were a sign of happy days to come for Raymond Domenech. Their comeback delighted us, but it annoyed me at the same time: the Zizoumania made it impossible for me to get all my friends and relatives tickets!

Anyway, I almost scored one of the most beautiful goals of my career with a volley that came pretty close to Grégory Coupet's goal. Never mind. The night belonged to Zidane and les Bleus (3–0). Sylvain Wiltord, hearing the racket coming from our changing rooms, whispered: 'Looks like you guys are having fun, got any space for me on the team?' There's always room for a talent like his . . .

Behind this special moment, however, defeat had shown us we'd have to tighten our form against the heavyweight teams.

Like Cameroon, who we faced on 4 September 2005 in a key game if we were to qualify for the World Cup.

We were in a good position, technically needing only a draw to get us to Germany. At Chelsea, Geremi kept going on about how they were going to overtake us – there was a major psychological battle between the Lions and the Elephants. The Cameroonians were messing around a bit but had managed to get things together before the final qualifiers in June.

We'd lost our advantage after drawing with Libya in June 2005 (0–0). That result put us in a critical position and we were exhausted. Towards the end of the season, our bodies were no longer responding. At least we hadn't actually lost, but we were miles away from the Lions.

On our way back from Tripoli, we'd been taken apart by the press. It was the first time I'd been on the receiving end of such criticism. In some newspaper, next to my name, it read: 'Very clumsy player. Must focus if he wants to avoid losing his spot.' I couldn't believe it! It made me chuckle but it got to me too . . . How could he write that when he probably hadn't even seen the match in Libya? Did he even know anything about football? He clearly didn't think of me as a striker, and I was pretty tense at the next press conference.

I'm always prepared to do these and my replies are honest. So this journalist comes to see me afterwards and asks me if I could answer a few more questions: I tell him I can't, so all of a sudden he gets aggressive: 'We're the ones who've got you this far and we can knock you down in a heartbeat.'

I threw back: 'Well hurry up then – if you got me where I am, I don't need you now – I'm the one putting food on your table.' It was a tense exchange. He went off and complained to my room-mate, Blaise Kouassi. 'Tell him we can shoot him down whenever we like!' The thing is, Blaise and I are joined at the hip, so he had a go at him and the guy came and apologised. I'd gone too far in the way I'd spoken to him but I hate it when people provoke me like that. We won against Egypt 2–0, with me scoring a double. That was my response – I buried all the critics. All that was left to do was to challenge Cameroon at home, against a backdrop of war and hope for reunification through football.

The start of my season hinged on that 4 September 2005 match. I couldn't stop thinking about it, about needing to get to the top that day, not wasting any of my energy before then, and most importantly not getting hurt. Our people were waiting for us, a nation was in agony, and badly in need of a dream.

We could sense this rare kind of passion surrounding us. After our victory against Egypt, people had filled the street. There was the same excitement as there'd been for Senegal in the knock-out stage of the 2002 World Cup in Japan and Korea. The same celebrations after each victory, the same madness – we were going from strength to strength and Cameroon was only two points ahead of us . . . With my experience and after my stint with Mourinho, I kept reminding myself that all we needed was a draw, even though beating them would have sent us straight to Germany one day before the end of the qualifiers.

The public and the management didn't see it that way: they could see us winning by three goals. So for a week, the pressure was very intense. The country was imagining us at the World Cup and the preparation was ridiculous. The Côte d'Ivoire needed peace and it was clinging on to its national team.

The only public moment of the week had been perplexing: we'd received a gift from a famous local politician, a huge painting featuring Cameroon's football players! It was a pretty thoughtless gesture, one that neither I nor the rest of the team particularly appreciated.

Before the encounter, the 'maquis', those little restaurants typical of the Côte d'Ivoire, had done great business. Beer and champagne flowed in a flurry of parties. Ivory Coast was going to the World Cup! We players were cloistered away in a wing of the Golf hotel, one of the largest hotels in Abidjan, amongst high-ranking members of the 'Forces Nouvelles' (New Forces), the name given to the former rebels, and UN soldiers. This landmark, where weapons were always in sight, was our protection from the city's turmoil.

I kept repeating the same thing over and over again like a mantra: 'We don't have to win.' The response tended to be 'Yes, we do.' The slogan on everyone's lips was 'We can either win, or we can win,' not a viewpoint that left much choice. The day before the confrontation saw some indescribable scenes in Abidjan, especially on the Rue Princesse, epicentre of African madness, where people partied before the game.

By morning, massive queues already blocked the city's main arteries, like orange snakes slithering towards the 'Felicia', as our stadium was nicknamed. 'This is our day of days,' you'd hear people saying with an almost biblical seriousness – meaning that we were dead certs to qualify. Abidjan held its breath; everyone was waiting for this match, both in Africa and elsewhere. José Mourinho had asked me if it was OK to come and attend the event, if it wasn't dangerous in light of the stories circulating in the media.

– Of course it's safe, come along, bring the president even!

– I don't know about that, he's never been to Africa.

– You've got to come, it'll be great. You won't be sorry when you feel the atmosphere.

They rose to the challenge. Roman Abramovich chartered his private jet. Abramovich and Mourinho in Abidjan! I was pleased to be able to show them my country, my home town, away from all the clichés spread by the press. When the PA announced their arrival, the stadium, which had been packed out since the morning, simply erupted. The Ivorians were chanting their names, the stands echoing back and forth for several minutes. It was hugely impressive, a truly historical moment.

Mourinho has often teased me about that: 'I am the King of Côte d'Ivoire. I'm a god over there. I never knew I was so revered.'

I'd retort: 'Of course you are but that's because I'm here. If I wasn't, they'd forget all about you!' At any rate, he witnessed and understood just how much the selection meant to me. Abramovich did too, but he and I didn't get a chance to talk about this special moment.

It was like a Champions League meeting. I was used to it and it made no difference to my preparation – to me it was nothing but another high-level match. The high stakes didn't worry or inhibit me. I tried to make my experience count; I knew success would come from Dindane, Kalou and me, because the Cameroon defence wasn't the best. Unfortunately, our defence failed. I scored two goals, one of them with a free kick, and thought we were heading for a draw and qualification. But Artur Jorge, our opponents' Portuguese trainer, anticipated the situation and blocked us strategically.

We deserved this defeat, even if it was late in coming (3–2). We stayed in the changing rooms a long time; an eternity. An hour, two hours, I don't even know. Some guys were crying their eyes out, crushed, broken. I'd never seen such desolation in that place and Yannick Noah, who was Cameroon's psychological coach, later confessed that he'd never felt such emotion coming from the other side of the wall.

The momentum had suddenly dropped, the Cup was slipping away from us. We were one point behind Cameroon, who were set to greet Egypt for the final encounter.

The mood at our hotel that night was pretty depressed. I popped into the disco, obviously not to have a dance but just to talk, to let it all out. Thierno Seydi, my agent, was there, as were some friends. I saw Arthur Boka, Didier Zokora pacing around the lobby. You just don't feel like going to bed at times like these, don't feel like sleeping. We were analysing the match over and over again. I was also annoyed at the criticism our goalkeeper Gérard Gnanhouan got, from Henri Michel especially.

He might well have fluffed his chance, but that can happen at the most crucial of times. He'd just fallen apart – I knew he could be decisive, as I'd seen him at Guingamp. We would just have to console ourselves with the African Cup in Egypt. We had to take this experience on board and go back to our clubs. And see my friend Geremi again, at Chelsea . . .

There was one last trip, which was to Sudan. We told ourselves: 'We can't not go.' There was one encouraging omen just before the trip – Geremi had been suspended. My team-mate was a model, a key player for the Lions Indomptables. Also Mido, my former OM teammate, had called me as we were getting ready for Egypt and assured me that his team would give it their all. 'Didier, Cameroon isn't going to win,' he'd assured me, confidently.

Sixteen of us left for Sudan – at least we were getting another match. Some had declined; they didn't believe we'd qualify and wanted to save themselves the hassle . . . Once we got to Sudan, we nicknamed ourselves the commando team. At the meeting, Sidy Diallo, who was the vice-president of the federation, warned us: 'If Cameroon makes a mistake and we still don't win, we may as well shoot ourselves in the head!' The heat was even more stifling than before in Abidjan, which is saying something – it was almost 50 degrees. I'd never experienced such conditions. At one point I wondered: 'What am I even doing here?' Despite the words being spoken, the details and declarations, our preparation felt more like a holiday.

On D-Day, Didier Zokora, aka Maestro, started going on about his visions. He kept shouting all over the hotel: 'I've had a vision of happiness! Today's the day!' Shut up Maestro, just give it a break! Still, he seemed pretty sure of himself . . . We got to the stadium, Henri Michel reminded us of the ground rules: 'No regrets. We're here to win. This may be our last chance, but we have to grab it!' That was exactly our state of mind. With every goal scored we just went back to work without celebrating (3–1 in the end). We got the job done, and that was that. To tell the truth we were pretty disillusioned. Suddenly my friend Cédric Degruson, who follows the Elephants around everywhere, camera in hand, broke in. He was on the phone to some staff guy who'd stayed behind in Paris. 'Draw! Two minutes left guys. Two minutes!'

Amazing. We huddled up together, unable to believe it. Cédric, what's the score? Still a draw. We've made it to Germany! 'Penalty!' What? 'Penalty for Cameroon!' And that was it. Over. I felt shattered. 'Come on, let's pray. Pray!' screamed Sidy Diallo. I'd had it, I was already feeling the elimination. 'Come on Didier, let's do it, pray.' I was pretty close to just walking away. It was too hard, to go out so close to our goal. We had no access to TV, nothing to hold on to.

'No way, they've missed!' Cédric shouted. Everyone was trying to get a word in, unable to stay still. Kolo Touré insisted: 'Steady guys!' I added: 'It's not over yet.' Others were praying, still. You can imagine how this ended, the ball close to the Egyptians' end . . . Cédric bursting: 'Over!' I broke into a sprint like never in my life, Carl Lewis-style, and ran over to hug Henri Michel. As I embraced him, I said: 'Thank you Henri.' I'll never take that away from him: he'd come to get the team qualified and he'd achieved it. We'd got heckled in Abidjan after losing against Cameroon, especially by the staff who'd always believed in us. I was amongst those who'd supported Henri through times of uncertainty. I didn't always see eye to eye with him, especially after those harsh words about Gnanhouan, like I've said before. But I couldn't fault him; he just had this style that was out of sync with what I was doing at Chelsea, with Mourinho. But he'd had a hunch about the game, had asked us to give the Elephants' swansong all we had: he'd had intuition, which is a great quality to have.

So we'd made it into the World Cup. The commando team had done it, but behind our success, there was also a whole nation in suffering, to whom we were bringing incommensurable joy. Three years of war, a country split in half . . .

With every match we saw our victories helping to cauterise wounds, ease tensions. We knew that in the northern part of the country we were heroes too; they'd pile in front of their TV sets to support us, erupting in celebration after our exploits. This victory belonged to a country reunited. We had to come together to take this joy further. What could we do to help put out this fire? We came up with the idea of sending out a peaceful message, one of hope.

Facing the cameras of the Ivorian national channel, Radio Télévision Ivoirienne, I spoke on behalf of the team, as the captain but above all as a child of the country. My teammates knew my intentions; we'd talked about this and I needed to speak out. It all felt natural, even though I did stumble on my words a little. I knew that the things I said carried a certain weight, that I would be heard. I felt like I was being listened to; it was a peaceful weapon that had to be used.

The message rang almost louder than the victory. I grabbed the mike, the guys gathered around me. I started with this knot in my stomach, a tightness in my chest, my emotions rife: 'All players please come together. Ivorians, men and women, from the north and the south, the centre and the west, you've seen this. We've proven to you that the people of Côte d'Ivoire can all live together side by side, play together towards one same goal: qualifying for the World Cup. We'd promised you this celebration would bring the people together. Now we're asking you to make this a reality. Please, let's all kneel.' There was a pause; we knelt. 'The only country in Africa with such wealth cannot sink into war like this. Please, put down your weapons, organise the elections and things will get better.'

Laughter gave way to tears. We'd gone through everything in one match, which seemed to sum up the whole tournament. An invisible thread linked the hearts of this commando group with one certainty: this qualification had got the crisis out of a rut; it had eased tensions and feelings of resentment in such difficult times. Everyone was talking about the end of the presidential term and troubles to come – we could go back to Abidjan both euphoric and mentally worn out.

On the return flight chartered by Laurent Gbagbo, the head of state, for the occasion, I suddenly felt overcome by emotions and wept, not even trying to hold back the tears – tears that held so many memories. I saw my whole life in pictures unreeling before my eyes: me at the airport, a small pouch hanging around my neck, five years old. One face in particular, haunting me. The beautiful face of a woman, her features filled with wisdom. Bea, the old one, as we say back home, my father's mother, gone too soon to see me there, in the headlines. I would have so loved for her to be by my side, she would have been so proud of me . . .

Landing in Abidjan. Madness. I am reunited with my parents, we embrace. Trying to contain this huge emotion. I want to hold them so tight, crush them almost. Thank you for everything, thank you for bringing me into this world, for bringing me up so well. It all happens so fast at times like these.

A throng awaits us – hundreds of thousands of people cram the streets. We're perched on the roof of a bus, unable to believe our eyes – under the burning sun, it takes almost four hours to reach the president's residence instead of the usual twenty. What a welcome – a crowd of happy faces, our bus drowning in the mêlée. We're making them feel so proud of being Ivorian, shattering all the clichés of a divided country.

These are people who have been waiting so long just to see us, to touch us – we all play for big clubs in Europe and they have few chances to get near us. These magical moments give them joy. This return to Abidjan let us believe that tensions were winding down. Our team was at an all-time high. It was also a victory for Anouma, who had given us the best conditions right from the start: private jets, sometimes, high-end hotels. The president had handed us the keys to success.

I've never had any problems at those gatherings, except a few classic money disputes, and of course our never-ending meetings. Still, when I hear of travelling to impossible countries, when I hear former players tell off-putting stories, I must admit I've never come across any of that. Nor have I ever run into the superstition that African teams are supposed to be riddled with.

Jean-Jacques Tizié, our old goalkeeper whom we used to call 'the shepherd', told us how before a match the players used to walk through cemeteries to chase away evil spirits, to help put their minds at rest. I'd seen stories on TV about Cameroon and its incredible ceremonies: these were a mystery to me. I would never have got picked in those conditions – it's just not my style, although we do have a whole bunch of beliefs. For a while, we prayed as Christians, and then later our prayers began to lean towards Islam. This blending of faiths helped us to grow, to reach this madness of October 2005. For the Ivorians, there is a before and an after Sudan. In our own way, we wrote a chapter of their lives and we're proud of that.

15

THE DAY I NEARLY GAVE
IT ALL UP . . .

Germany 2006 – sad memories. I passed through the World Cup like a shadow. I'd just finished a whirl-wind season with Chelsea, and given how we'd fared in the African Cup of Nations in Egypt in January and February, I thought our team was in with a chance. This ACN, which we lost to the host country in the final, had opened up some fine prospects and served as a wake-up call. We tended to waver for ten or fifteen minutes after each goal, which made us vulnerable, so we had to work on our concentration and keep our excitement under control. We had flaws to correct and the continental trial showed we'd made real progress – we'd found a kind of balance, with the team no longer split in two. For a long time, our style only really shone through when we had the ball, so we needed to find a strike force during recovery time, and pairing up Yaya Touré and Zokora in Cairo provided relief. We felt confident in our record as we arrived in Germany.

Argentina, Serbia, the Netherlands, the so-called 'Group of Death' didn't scare me. I had thought about it before the game: there were only seven matches between us and glory, so why not us? Why not believe in our chances and become the first African country to lift the Cup? Henri Michel had tried to bring the team back down to earth at the first press conference in Hamburg before the opening match against Argentina (lost 2–1). He obviously didn't see us as favourites – we lacked the experience. It seemed as if he would be content with getting through the qualifiers.

I didn't feel that way: when I enter a competition, I aim for the top prize – nothing less. After that, events may settle the score, but nothing should ever hold back your ambition from the outset.

Unfortunately, right from the training phase in Vittel, I knew we'd got off on the wrong foot. I can still see myself moaning at our hotel, in this spa town, feeling the World Cup, my first ever, slip out of reach.

The physical training didn't suit the condition I was in – I needed action, to work on my speed of execution, my start and reaction speed, and all we did were longer runs, 300, 200, 150 metres. I kept on at our coach, Roger Propos, about it but it made no difference. What bothered me was that he was following the same protocol with Côte d'Ivoire as with

Marseille, which was where we had met. But there was a huge difference: you can't manage a player the same way at the end of a season as at the start – I was so tired of wearing myself out running.

You've got to adapt the training to suit the situation – you can't just rely on textbook knowledge. Even though the work done before the ACN was good, it wasn't right any more. You need to know how to listen to the players, to their feelings, especially when they talk to you and express their needs. I wasn't trying to big myself up and impose myself as the trainer, but my years as a professional player have made me aware of my strengths and weaknesses – I now know more about my body and how it will react to the work. Roger and I didn't get along, but that didn't stop me believing in our team, in our strike force. I scored our country's first-ever World Cup goal against Argentina but I felt leaden. Drained.

I wasn't ready. This feeling never once left me, from training right through to the time I left Germany. I weighed a ton, I couldn't get my speed up, lacked get up and go. And to think that three weeks earlier I was flying like a butterfly in my Blues shirt . . . I tallied two yellow cards in as many matches, and that was the end of my competition after our defeat against the Netherlands (2–1). I made do with supporting my teammates against Serbia (3–2) and watching them achieve the Elephants' first victory in this tournament. We could have done better, I'm sure of it.

Sadly, it wasn't the ACN team that took part in Germany. I was laid low by mounting problems throughout the competition, but my physical condition was almost secondary. In Egypt we had a team that worked, but in the World Cup egos started cropping up. Everyone wanted to snatch their own piece of glory. What had happened to our solidarity, our much vaunted team spirit that everyone talked about? It was vanishing at the worst possible time, during the biggest test of all . . . This individualism was harming the team – some players more than others. I had a status to maintain, and this kind of failure wasn't going to do anything for my reputation.

In Cairo, I had the impression everyone was with me, following my lead. Here, I felt it was a bit every-man-for-himself. I sensed jealousy – was it my fault? People would bring up the Côte d'Ivoire and my name kept cropping up in the media. We'd see this ad on German television screens for Chocolat du Planteur, a symbol of our country, with me as their face. So what? What was the problem? When they talked about me, they were talking about the Côte d'Ivoire. I wasn't the only winner in all this media flurry. If some players have now made it to major clubs, it's obviously thanks to their abilities, but it's also because I gave my all as a striker. Just like Aruna Dindane.

We'd taken Côte d'Ivoire to top billing and it wasn't a selfish thing. It was a human, collective endeavour, and I had nothing to gain on an individual level. I had a run-in with Yaya Touré during some video, but even that was to do with football. Still, I was disappointed because I was trying to play my part as captain, putting myself on the line. I thought everyone else shared my state of mind. How wrong I was.

At that point I don't think Yaya could see where I was coming from, but he's somebody who's able to analyse a situation and eventually he got it. I'm glad, even though it took a while, even if it came a little late. He's still young. Also, we're different people with different ways of expressing ourselves.

Maybe I should have found a different way of explaining what I wanted. Those events took it out of me, and I didn't want to get myself involved in the ridiculous squabbles that went on among some of the academicians from ASEC, protected by Jean-Marc Guillou* and others. That wasn't a concern to me. The only problem was in the players' heads: individualism was winning out against team spirit. After the defeat against the Netherlands in Stuttgart (2–1), Peter Kenyon had come to see me – I was fed up, and spent a long time in my hotel room mulling over this failure. A dream had fallen apart and just one thought kept going through my mind: to leave the squad. I wanted to announce my decision straight away – if I was a problem for the others, I had to take responsibility and go.

This World Cup could have been a time of pure joy, but it turned into a nightmare – a real disappointment, from both a sporting and human perspective. I felt that people were bothered by me, that I wasn't welcome in the team. I didn't

* Jean-Marc Guillou is a former star player who won 19 caps for the French team and went on to create a football academy in Abidjan which produced a large number of today's international players.

realise, but, it turned out the buzz I generated wasn't to everyone's taste. My success made them uncomfortable, and I was harming the Elephants. I didn't want to put a brake on the team's development.

Maybe I had to think about doing something else, devote myself to my club. I wasn't acting out of spite. I could have made my decision on the spot, right after we were knocked out. In the end I thought it through, weighed all the pros and cons, spoke to friends and family. It wasn't a snap decision – I really wanted to pack it all in. Still, I let almost two months go by before I mentioned it to Jacques Anouma, the president of the federation. This wasn't just some careless response to the disappointment of being knocked out of the World Cup, to hitting a low point. The president, who I greatly respect, convinced me to stay with the Elephants, telling me I was his main man and he didn't want me to leave. I couldn't do it. We'd been through so much together, so much joy. 'If there are issues to sort out, we'll sort them out,' he assured me.

I was his captain – no way we were going to let each other down. We had started this adventure and we were going to see it through together. Somehow, I bit the bullet for the president because of all he'd done for me. I owed him one for believing in me as a Guingamp substitute.

I also started up a dialogue with certain teammates: their feelings mattered too. They looked at me differently and I found this a change for the worse. It took me a while to get back into the groove and up to speed. My state of mind wasn't the same as before. I was part of the team, I played but I was detached, still reeling from a serious blow; I'm an emotional person. And then, as the months went by, my enthusiasm came back, and most of all, relationships returned to normal. The group matured, something which had to happen, and these days I think I'd have made a big mistake if I'd walked out on this fantastic human adventure.

I love that shirt – I wear it like a second skin, its shield on my heart, a lifelong passion. When I was starting out, as soon as I'd get the fax summoning me, I'd run to buy my flight. It was like a breath of pure oxygen. Even so, I did almost quit: looking back, I would have found it hard to cope with the frustration of not seeing it through to the end. With that team, with the Ivorian people.

I have high hopes for 2010 if we can commit to a common goal. I think young people got my message and what it meant. No African team has ever won the World Cup. The trophy is ours to win in South Africa, on our soil. It's worth fighting for, worth keeping those egos in check. The whole continent will be watching and cheering us on. Of course, we need to qualify first, but I only ever imagine the best, never the worst. After that, anything is possible. Seven matches. As I said before playing Argentina in Hamburg, what are seven matches in a career? Just a drop in the ocean.

Four years between Germany and South Africa. I was so close to quitting the Elephants in 2006, I'd love to be the one lifting the Cup to the blue Johannesburg sky, proving I am an African at heart. So, I'll see you in Joburg . . .

16

AFRICA DENIED

My love affair with African football has yet to be consummated. I've been through two African Cups of Nations and have always come out the other end feeling like I hadn't quite finished the job, or somehow unfulfilled. Whether in Egypt, in 2006, when the host country stopped us in the final (0–0, 4–2 after penalties), or in Ghana, two years later, when our hopes were snuffed in the semi-final by those same Pharaohs (4–1), we've seen this trophy we so coveted slip through our hands. The tournament in Ghana was my biggest disappointment, because then we really had what it takes to beat the odds.

In Cairo, we lost our final match on penalties, and this knife-edge failure had given us reason to hope. We'd come out of this competition feeling really strong after beating Cameroon and Nigeria. Our quarter-final against the Lions Indomptables of Cameroon was intense, as it took twelve penalties before a winner emerged. I had to take two shots in this strange exercise, not something that happens often.

I didn't particularly appreciate the way this meeting between Samuel Eto'o and me was touted in terms of rivalry: there were no grounds for that at all. We may well have been the two best African strikers of the day, but I'm no one's rival. Samuel and I share a common goal: we want to put our continent on top. That's what matters to us the most.

The final against Egypt taught me that the prize is never easily won on the host's home turf. We'd had to contend with a classic sabotage tactic: our coach was blocked for forty-five minutes just yards from the stadium thanks to a bunch of crazed fans. It wasn't so much intimidation as a way of show-ing off – intimidation was what you got in the suburbs of Paris, when you played in the midst of tower blocks and guys with dogs ready to pounce would stand on the edge of the pitch threatening: 'If you don't get off the ball we're letting them loose.' So really, by comparison, getting stuck on a coach outside some stadium is a schoolboy prank . . .

This Cup had to stay in Egypt; it was important to the country at that point in time. Anyway, the Pharaohs weren't undeserving, they had the best team and they went on to prove it two years later in Accra.

For me this second defeat against them came as a huge slap in the face, even more so with the match being played so close to home, in a neighbouring country. Our group had never felt so close-knit, so together, mature, individually and as a team. After our victories over Nigeria (1–0) then Guinea (5–0) in the quarter-finals, we thought we had things under control; we were playing by the rules, getting on well. Unfortunately, we failed to solve the problem set by our opponents, masters in the art of controlling space: failing to react, Ivory Coast had no solution. We were there in spirit, less so tactically. Were we victims of our youth? When talking about the Elephants, people often forget our lack of experience. Maybe we got ahead of ourselves, picturing ourselves too soon in the finals, especially after our blinding victory over the Guineans. And to think we'd been planning to get our revenge over Egypt . . . Not quite.

Most observers saw us as dead certs to pick up the Cup. At our hotel in Takoradi, in the western part of Ghana, we'd been able to prepare in the best possible conditions, away from any turmoil. Visits were limited to the bare minimum and I'd asked the security officer to filter my meetings with people. Every day people wanted to talk to me – our fans had travelled en masse.

Some of them claimed to be saving their money for their ticket to the final, but they were to be disappointed.

This competition was marred by the death of the son of Ulrich Stielike, our coach. At the last minute, right before our preparation stage, the German left Gérard Gili in charge so he could go to his seriously ill child's sickbed. Before the ACN in

Egypt, it had been the death of one of our friend and team-mate Aruna Dindane's little girls that devastated us, and obviously grief affected us – how could it not?

For my part, I experienced a rare thing. I knew that football could sometimes be thankless, but I'd never faced anything as tough as this. The scene unfolded on Friday 1 February, two days before our quarter-final.

The African Confederation (CAF) had decided to organise an awards ceremony for player of the year in Lomé, Togo, a country bordering Ghana, right in the middle of the tournament. I was lying on my bed in my hotel room when the phone rang; the official sponsor asked me if there was any chance I could make it to the party. I could understand him wanting to gather all the recipients together, but why couldn't he have held the event on a different date?

I've already told you about the internal problems my overexposure caused at the World Cup, and I didn't want to make things worse. The Ivorian federation didn't want to see one of its players leave so close to a crucial match and I wasn't about to make that decision on my own, so I couldn't go.

I was asked to speak to Habuba, the CAF's press officer, who told me it would be good for me to show up, and then passed me to Issa Hayatou, the president, who insisted and warned me: 'We've had to call an emergency crisis meeting of the CAF executive committee and they've agreed that as of this afternoon, if the winner of the trophy fails to attend the ceremony, the prize will go to the runner-up.' He also assured me that he had his eyes on Côte d'Ivoire . . . I was gob-smacked. He spoke very calmly, never raising his voice, giving off this genuine power, this quiet authority.

They asked Frédéric Kanouté, the future winner, to attend, but if Mali made it to the quarter-finals, Jean-François Jodar, its selector, had already stated that he wasn't willing to travel. I said I was prepared to send my wife but she obviously wasn't welcome there. Strange tactics. They didn't want her to collect the trophy on my behalf, which hit me hard because it meant a lot to me.

I could have got a second consecutive award, a dream come true for any Ivorian, but instead I was brought crashing down to earth.

I can't make sense of the CAF's attitude. I'd just finished fourth in the *France Football* Ballon d'Or, I'd done well in the FIFA listings, and I was hoping for this continental accolade. I wouldn't have been bothered if I lost: it'd happened in 2005, against Eto'o. My frustration mostly stemmed from how it was done – I was being denied a victory as punishment for not travelling to Togo, which showed a complete lack of respect, an abuse of power on CAF's part.

This is a title awarded on the basis of votes from coaches and the media committee, so it seemed as though they were changing the rules as they went along. Does an actor have to be present at the Oscars to earn his prize? I doubt it . . .

After that business, I couldn't sleep a wink. I felt as if I was caught up in political wrangling between Hayatou and Jacques

Anouma, president of the Ivorian federation and his one-time opponent. I could see myself become entangled in a kind of settling of scores.

I was tired before the match against Guinea, but I'd pulled myself together – as captain, I couldn't let my weaknesses show to the group. I tried to hide my emotions but are they really something that can be controlled? I found that I couldn't – I didn't feel right and I think this episode had something to do with it.

I almost didn't play in the quarter-final. Seeing the state I was in in the dressing room, the staff called Pascal, someone you will come across later in the book. He showed up a few minutes before kick-off and tried to calm me down but it wasn't happening. I was in a state – I felt awful, knocked out, sick to my stomach. A few minutes into the game, I was feeling so dreadful that I thought I'd have to leave the pitch. I was losing it, avoiding head-to-heads because I was losing twenty per cent of my energy at every impact. When Kader Keita, of Lyon, opened the scoring, I couldn't even congratulate him; I went and got some water from the bench instead. I was exhausted, played out.

Thankfully things got better in the second half – I scored and made a crucial pass. After my goal I struck a Cantona pose, my upper body straight, eyeing the crowd with haughty stares. I don't know why, perhaps it was a retort to all the madness that had surrounded me over the last few days. I managed fifteen minutes in that game, not a single one more.

Qualifying had settled me, as had the Ivorians' support –

they had understood my attitude. Right after that, the day after our victory I announced I was pulling out of the African Footballer of the Year competition, for good. I obviously couldn't stop people from voting for me, but the fact that I wouldn't travel ruled me out of contention, according to those new rules dictated on the tarmac of Accra airport . . .

This wasn't an easy decision to make. Never again will I experience the joy and pride I felt the year before. I called Freddie Kanouté afterwards because I didn't want him to appear winner by default. I really rate him and he deserved this accolade, just like Essien did.

It was the process I criticised, not a person. Kanouté is a smart guy and knew where I was coming from, and this story hasn't affected our friendship – he assured me of that.

So for now, Africa is brushing off my advances but the Elephants and I are impatiently waiting for the next time round, in Angola, 2010. This might be my last chance to win a major continental distinction, as part of a team. As an individual, never again.

17

THE POINTLESS WAR

The giant screen near the stairs is showing me unbearable images. At home in Guingamp I watch convoy after convoy of refugees, leaving northern Côte d'Ivoire, fleeing Bouaké, now the capital of the rebellion.

This could be a film about any other African tragedy. I can still see those millions of Ethiopians, Rwandans, Congolese, forced to walk for miles to escape the worst dangers. These children and women on rutted roads, cutting across fields, with no one but themselves to lean on . . . A nightmare. Why? How? These questions eat away at me – it's unbearable.

The Côte d'Ivoire, often considered the Switzerland of Africa, fell to war on the night of 18 September 2002, just a few days after I started against South Africa. It was terrible. I'd never imagined such a conflict could happen, never pictured such an explosion. An official in the national team had told me, though, some four or five months before the breakout, that there were serious social problems. 'Things are tense, people hardly speak to each other any more . . .' I hadn't noticed a thing, never imagined that this conflict would break out, but it didn't take long for reality to kick in.

Some friends of my father's were killed, and that's when you realise it isn't just a game. The pictures that darken your living room take on deeper meaning, even if you aren't directly hit.

My status shields me from misery; I'm not blind to that. I took on a role of peace ambassador because I wanted to help my country get out of this pit. This responsibility raised up our national team into a force able to break down obstacles and ease tensions. The team became a symbol of the reunification of Côte d'Ivoire.

But we're no politicians. All we can do is radiate positivism and give pacifist speeches; we don't have the power to stop wars. Sometimes this responsibility scared me, but we upheld our end of the bargain by qualifying for the World Cup. That was our contribution to peace.

I had a hard time with how the French media portrayed things, basically saying it was north against south, Christians against Muslims. How could they oversimplify so drastically? Anyone from the south was suddenly suspect, all Ivorians represented as xenophobic, tribalistic . . . A tough thing for such open, hospitable people to accept.

Africa's problems are so often analysed simplistically, pinning everything on ethnicity, forgetting that our societies are getting younger and less and less based on ethnic groups. If you walked into one of Abidjan's town halls on a Saturday, you'd be surprised at the number of mixed marriages being celebrated.

I couldn't understand how they could depict the conflict like that – what a sad state of affairs. Luckily, the national team was the absolute antithesis – there was no way we could suffer the same divisions because here, people from all religions just had to get along. My goal-scoring pairing with Aruna Dindane is itself a symbol for tolerance, with him coming from Burkina Faso and me a 'bété' (from the western Ivory Coast). As if two groups couldn't accept each other . . . anyway, who wouldn't get on with Aruna? We'd never before heard anyone talk about Ivorian nationalism, let alone civil war . . . Politicians used those themes for their own ends, leaving the country burnt and bleeding. Opinions were manipulated, especially through the media.

Obviously, the Côte d'Ivoire can't compete in terms of putting out information with the international papers sold at airports around the world. What is written becomes reality. How could *Fraternité Matin*, our number one daily paper, even begin to matter when faced with such heavyweights?

Some journalists could have delved a little deeper into Ivorian society. Most of them seemed not to know much about it, as though working from Paris or tucked away cosily amongst friends in Abidjan. There was so much to discover in

Côte d'Ivoire, so much to see and learn. Too many of the news reports were biased and I would have liked to tell them so . . . At one point I just stopped reading, I stopped watching what French TV had to say about it.

In the typical, endlessly repeated analyses, I was always 'close to someone in power', as the president was 'bété' like me. Whenever I give my opinion, I try to be as objective as I can and not stick to one particular region or religion; I try to take a step back from it all. Is it normal to have to either hide or justify your culture just to get your views across? No one can pigeon-hole me anyway.

I am far from a stereotypical Ivorian: my wife is Malian and Muslim, my agent Senegalese. I have a weird relationship with religion. As a child I used to go to church and take Sunday school, and as I grew up, although I didn't attend so regularly I continued to believe, and when I reached 18 or 19 I started going to the mosque because my friends were all Muslim. I hung out with them out of curiosity, trying to understand why they'd chosen that religion and I had followed another path. I really liked some of the precepts of the Koran – I belong to a younger generation which is attracted to Islam: Nicolas Anelka, Freddie Kanouté, Philippe Christanval, Louis Saha . . . The most important thing isn't to be Muslim, Jewish or Christian, it's to believe in God and above all to respect people's differences.

So I didn't fit into the pre-established scheme of things, and I didn't talk about my beliefs, which are private. Only peace matters to me, so I felt really uncomfortable in the middle of all this drama, with the tension between my two countries.

People were actually protesting against Jacques Chirac's foreign policy – they weren't against the French on a personal level, and of course, I don't condone violence or losing it, but this was a patronising, neocolonial policy towards a country that has been independent since 1960. It's about time the Côte d'Ivoire was left to do its own growing up, make its own decisions about the future and its politicians. It isn't right for such a vision of our continent to persist.

The events of November 2004, with the death of nine French soldiers and about fifty Ivorian civilians killed by French military in front of the Hotel Ivoire, were terrible. They really got to me and we had to wait for a report from Canal+ before a lot of things became clear . . . What was the French government playing at? The official version couldn't hold up when faced with the images broadcast by the pay channel.

In Africa, this clash had a strong impact on young people, and not just in Côte d'Ivoire. Those civilian shootings were very traumatic, and despite my dual nationality, I was having a hard time taking France's side, even though I was touched by the departure of 8,000 of its citizens. Those people were as Ivorian as they were French and had built their life in the land of elephants, with many of them since returning. Those massacres in front of Hotel Ivoire gave rise to this anti-French phenomenon even though at base Ivorians had nothing at all against the French, and still don't. We're French-speakers, Abidjan is nicknamed 'Petit Paris' ('Little Paris'), young people still dream of the Champs-Elysées, although with time's passing and these tragic events, the USA has emerged as an alternative.

African countries and Côte d'Ivoire especially are important to France both strategically and economically, so I can understand how at some point its leaders might not have been open to emancipation, but the situation is infuriating because the people suffer and the damage is sometimes irreversible. I'm not pretending there are no social issues in Côte d'Ivoire – land disputes are what led to friction, and the fact that Côte d'Ivoire is a developing country plagued by high unemployment and substandard literacy has given rise to human disasters. We must try to understand the issues and solve them. Of course, we *will* solve them, together.

Honestly, my country has everything it needs to succeed – great people full of life, plenty of natural resources. I'm looking forward to the elections so this nightmare can come to an end and we can see the start of a new era for a more mature and self-assured Côte d'Ivoire. Everybody's tired, people have learned a lot about politics and international relations over these last few years, and I hope the time for peace has come at last. Between Ivorians. With France. These two countries have so much to give one another – I'm convinced of this. In fact I'm living proof: the midwife who brought me into the world was French; those hands that helped me out of my mother's womb were white. There is no stronger symbol.

Our countries are on the road back to normality. Right now, the climate favours warmer relations. The way it used to be.

18

MY ROOTS

The Côte d'Ivoire and France. France and the Côte d'Ivoire. The fusion of my two countries is what has made me who I am. These days, it might come across as though I'm going back to my African roots, nurturing ties I once neglected. Not so. I have never abandoned my past and I'm proud to be called Tébily, the middle name I was given in memory of my paternal grandfather. It helps me hold on to my origins, gives me this added strength.

I didn't spend long in my native country, but my memories of it never fade. They have helped me remember what's essential. Oddly, it is easier for me to picture Abidjan than Brest or Angoulême, these cities I passed through with my uncle. My years before becoming an expat bring to life their own batch of memories. I almost feel as though I left paradise on earth. I have never regained the same sense of freedom I felt in the Côte d'Ivoire, with the fun we had after a day at school, those football games, getting up to no good as children do. As a person who has never dealt well with constraints or prohibitions, I felt happy there: kind of left to my own devices. This is how I learnt to become me.

As a child, I often travelled with my father. I can still see those colours that remind me of Africa, bring back those smells you wouldn't find anywhere else. Like the aroma of the cocoa the Côte d'Ivoire is the world's number one producer of, wafting along the Giscard d'Estaing Boulevard which leads to Abidjan airport. Like the scent of the earth during the rainy season. The heat, the water combining to create this wonderful blend that's so hard to resist. As children we would take advantage of cloudbursts to take warm showers, dripping with happiness.

The red tracks, this ochre soil, the noise of communal courtyards still assail my memory. My African roots are strong – they run deep, and each return to the country brings them back to the surface.

I need to come back at regular intervals, to recharge my batteries. For a long time, I couldn't afford to go back as often as I would have liked to, but those days are over. I found it hard to be so far away – I was homesick. Like I said earlier in the book, leaving your family isn't an easy thing to do.

When I was a child, at my uncle's place in France, my home continent made itself known to me through music, first and foremost. In the car on the weekend, he would put on a Sam Fan Thomas tape, or Aurlus Mabélé or Kassav and it would take me far away . . . Straight to Africa! The same happened when we had get-togethers with friends or went to birthday parties, where we would dance like crazy – I couldn't stop moving and shaking that long body of mine. It was like a breath of fresh air. As the years went by, even my aunt, who is from Brittany, soaked up the local culture. The more time passed, the more she'd swap steak with pasta, or *bœuf bourguignon* with fries, for African dishes in hearty sauces. Africa got to her too.

How can I begin to explain the taste of a Lokossoukoué, my mother's speciality? This is the dish we usually had at get-togethers. Wonderful. It was mashed banana with a pretty strong, gloopy sauce made from black mushrooms, almonds, wild mango and dried fish. In place of forks, we would use the fingers of the right hand (in our tradition, the left hand is never used for eating, only lowly tasks) to scoop up and better savour this delight. Côte d'Ivoire abounds in these exquisite culinary treasures.

I feel I have a dual culture – I have never had to ask myself if I am more French or more Ivorian, as I am steeped in both traditions, a priceless gift. When I first arrived in Continental France, I felt that some things were missing – my ties to my roots were obviously stretched. In terms of pure tradition and deep bonds with the land, I am behind but catching up at my own pace. When it comes to small aspects of everyday life, like the way I speak, entertain myself, eat, I still felt completely Ivorian. Saying that, I don't speak my dialect, 'bété' very well, but I do understand it a little and I went back to my parents' villages in June 2007 – to Niaprahio, my father's village, and Guiberoha, my mother's, about 10 kilometres apart. This was easily more than fifteen years after the last time I visited, and this time in a convoy with a police escort heading off down the unsurfaced road through a tightly packed but welcoming crowd.

Of course, I wasn't able to savour those moments the way I had hoped to – I couldn't take those short cuts, hear the noises that came from another place, revisit my past on my own . . . I stayed for an hour or two, listened to the speeches, received gifts and tributes. It was like visiting a portrait, far removed from the intimacy of my youth.

Really, the feeling I get the second I land in Abidjan is something else – total bliss. At first, whenever I would leave the Côte d'Ivoire to go to Europe, I would feel a tightness in my chest as though reliving my first departure for Bordeaux, with my bag slung over my shoulder, the sorrow of my parents, my blankie in hand. My real return was my first selection for the Elephants against South Africa in September 2002 in Abidjan.

This was a revelation – I reconnected, despite not having that sense of belonging felt by other team members who had grown up there, and feeling a little lost. Music helped – I would borrow my friends' CDs, burn them and listen to them when back home in France. My mates made me feel comfortable and over time I began to feel the Ivorian vibe more strongly – the national team helped me get inside my new skin. With Bonaventure Kalou, we had even decided to celebrate our goals by dancing *coupé-décalé*, a popular dance in Abidjan. It was a bet we had – the one who'd score a goal would have to bust those jerky moves, a hand splitting the air: we both scored the following week and launched into these moves. Then it became a kind of tradition. At Marseille, then Chelsea. I had to laugh at some English or French teammates who would try to do it without ever really getting it right. They had a long way to go . . .

I realised that in all those Elephants gatherings, we had something in common – I won't even start on the problems we had with timekeeping, or perhaps a certain 'nonchalance'. This is a term we often heard from our coaches' mouths when I first started out – Alain Pascalou especially found my laid-back attitude annoying.

I know this is something that gets to Europeans who mistake our apparent tranquillity for provocation, but that's not what it is. The African man feels strong, untouchable. He doesn't ever doubt, always aims higher. Life has taught him this art of thinking, of reacting. It isn't pretension, just an innate strength of character. In the light of the problems our countries have, we have developed a huge capacity for adaptation. When you leave at a young age, or leave behind your family to seek your fortune elsewhere, it forges a state of mind. Psychologically, Africans are very strong – they know how to stay cheerful even through the hard times, and stay looking relaxed on the outside. In Côte d'Ivoire, for instance, the country found itself in an unprecedented crisis which could have nipped any desire to party in the bud. This never happened.

In the streets, in the 'maquis', you constantly see people having fun – they know how to forget and live in the moment. In our culture, one of the first things we are taught is never to complain and to make do with the happiness we are given, no matter how scarce. This makes sense when you see how many people pass away, leaving us while still in their prime – death is a faithful travel companion, and I still carry within me this slightly fatalistic Ivorian mentality. The idea is that at the end of the day 'things will be OK', that there is always a glimmer of hope. Africans often reckon that things will be better tomorrow and they have all the time in the world, but this strong belief in their destiny means they are sometimes blinded by their faith. This great strength of character can turn against them because it sometimes masks reality. This is what happened at the beginning of my career when I kept misbehaving and thinking I was immune to everything, until I finally realised that this nonchalance was bordering on recklessness. Age has made me wiser.

I understood that I had a lot to gain by planning for the future rather than living for the moment. In Africa, we often get stuck in the present, unsurprisingly – such idiosyncrasies stem from our way of life, the difficulties of life which stop you thinking too far ahead. No way would you miss out on good times, fall victim to pessimism. I don't know a single Ivorian who doesn't love to have fun . . . We'd rather escape than go mumble in a corner. My fellow countrymen are anything but loners.

From childhood, we are accustomed to being around people, 'tantis', 'old folk', which are terms of respect that refer to our relations. To be called 'old' is an honour; I'm not so sure that that's the case in France . . .

Anyway, when you share your home with a lot of people, you get so used to this constant supply of everyday human warmth that it makes it hard to enjoy being alone. I travelled around Africa quite a lot and I found some similarities with the Côte d'Ivoire in people's eyes, in the way they live.

Those trips are worth so much to me. Like the time I trekked around the Island of Gorée, off the coast of Senegal. I would advise anyone to visit this scrap of land, testament to a past era. This is a place millions of black people left, were deported from to build a new world, far from home with their lives destroyed. When you are there, history grips you, emotions take you over. The curator of the island took me to see the house of slaves and the museum. I saw the door of no return, an opening towards a sea which would lead them to a grim horizon. After embarking on those giant cemeteries, many of them died at sea and were flung overboard like trash.

For all these reasons, both as a person and a sportsman, winning the African 'ballon d'or' in 2007 meant a great deal to me. Before I went to Ghana, which is where I was awarded this prize, I wondered: am I going to be chosen, at long last, or will I have to make do with runner-up? I decided to travel to Accra without really knowing anything, without knowing the result, with Michael Essien, my mate from Chelsea, in a private jet. I only found out the rankings at the last minute, and when I went backstage and saw my mother looking so beautiful, when I put on a traditional 'Kita' loincloth, I just knew the prize was mine. My mother was so proud of her boy she was dancing, kissing me. I felt so happy for the Côte d'Ivoire.

I was breaking Samuel Eto'o's record, who had been chosen three times in a row. Zinédine Zidane once said: 'With football, you need to leave your mark, achieve things that become engraved in history.' In my own way, I was making my mark in my country's history. I was the first Elephant ever to win a personal trophy when Pokou, Abdoulaye Traoré, Youssouf Fofana and so many others had preceded me in the pantheon of national football heroes. This crown propelled me into the exclusive circle of great continental talents: Eto'o, Weah, Okocha, Diouf . . . Huge. They paved the way. For many, football has become an escape from dire living conditions. We are, in our own way, emblems for our generation just like Abédi Pelé, George Weah, Laurent Pokou once were. Who in Africa hasn't known those bundles of cloth, plastic bags rolled into a ball? How many children are there who got to dream of magic destinies and 'golden footballs' while kicking around these hand-made toys?

Africa will only be truly respected within the world of football once European clubs agree to release their players as readily for the African Cup of Nations as for the European Championships. As our continental competition takes place from mid-January to mid-February, our clubs are obliged to give us two weeks off before the tournament starts, but a lot of them exert unacceptable pressure. There is a calendar and there are rules, and the teams know it – this is how Freddie Kanouté, who had just opted for Malian nationality, got blackmailed by Tottenham: 'If you go to the ACN, we won't let you play again!' When he came back, he had to look for something else because he was no longer included in the coach's plans. He had become a luxury stand-in despite being the best striker in the club before his departure. A sad episode indeed.

We know that being African is hardly an advantage. All things being equal, an African will earn less than a European or South American player, even with advertising contracts. It happened to me in the past but not any more. I learned to demand respect.

The rise of high-level Africans is going to break down this ethnocentric vision of things. It may be necessary to review the dates of the ACN, to bring the tournament forward a little, but nobody will stop us from representing our country. Never. José Mourinho wouldn't have tried to affect my decision – before the 2006 ACN in Egypt he would joke: 'You're off on holiday. You'd better come back well rested!' This was his way of telling me he would have liked me to stay. Then he changed his tune. After we beat Cameroon in the penalty shoot-out in the quarter-final he wished me luck: 'Now you've got to win this, we're right behind you!'

This tournament means so much in our countries; it causes

such a magnificent outpouring of emotion, changes destinies. Matches bring life to a standstill, transform countries.

The Black–White–Arab phenomenon took France by storm after the 1998 World Cup victory and gathered a tremendous following. Even for a brief moment, it brought these people together. We know the limitations of these movements but we also know their reach, despite being isolated events, and even when they are nothing but symbolic. The same applies to us – they bring happiness, and this occasionally over-the-top passion is a part of us, of our culture, our history. It is a part of me.

19

MY OTHER WORLD

I used to be Didier. Now I'm Drogba. At Le Mans, at Guingamp, people used to call me by my first name – I was their mate. Those days are over – people look at me differently now.

As Fabrice, my childhood friend from the Baconnets estate in Antony, said, laughing: 'Do you remember when we used to scrounge francs off people in the street to buy a slice of pizza?' We were at my place, in a posh part of west London. More of a town, really – a peaceful, reassuring place full of celebrities. Apparently Cliff Richard and Tom Jones live nearby, and John Lennon and Ringo Starr used to own houses around the corner. Not bad for a kid from Yopougon, the working-class district of Abidjan . . .

Of course I remember, Fabrice – I haven't forgotten a thing. Not the one room the whole family used to cram into in Levallois. Not the stories we used to tell as kids, those fantasies we invented, the lives we dreamt up. I have never forgotten that in my heart of hearts I always knew that one day I'd make it big. Despite all the obstacles, despite the sarcasm, despite my mates who used to mock my trips from Antony to Levallois just to kick a ball around. It was all worth it in the end, wasn't it, guys?

How could I forget? It's a pleasure to revisit my past, my amazing career.

One memory in particular brings it all back. The first time I saw myself on posters in Paris I couldn't believe it. My face for all the world to see in the Métro I so often took to training as a kid. It was really me. Didier Drogba, never destined to be a star. I was deliriously happy. Who knew where I had come from? Me, my family and now you. It was really something – the party animal of yesterday had come of age. No longer was I the teenager tiptoeing into the apartment in Antony, trying not to wake my parents, not always successfully. Sometimes I would barely make it to my room before I heard, 'We're off shopping!' To Saint-Denis, without a car and without a minute's sleep. Almost an order – an hour to get there, an hour to get back. That was my life, so far from where I am today.

Since then I've met my fair share of the good and the great. In 2004, Laurent Gbagbo, the president of the Côte d'Ivoire, asked to meet me when he was passing through Paris, but I was playing away with OM in Montpellier. I sent him a football kit. After that I met him often in Abidjan with the Elephants, as well as Guillaume Soro, the Côte d'Ivoire's prime minister after the uprising. I presented my African ballon d'or to him in his fiefdom of Bouaké: in my own way I acted as kind of a gateway to peace, without ever getting mixed up in politics. That wasn't my role, although like any other citizen I had my own point of view.

Football has opened up the doors of fame, broadened my horizons. I've had the honour of sharing the precious time of Amadou Toumani Touré, president of Mali, Abdoulaye Wade, president of Senegal, and so many other famous figures. Meeting these heads of state is no trivial thing: it is a gift, a privilege.

I want to make the most of everything that comes my way. Imagine a music fan like me, nicknamed Tupac by Kader Seydi in my years at Le Mans, in front of Snoop Dogg, US rapper, universal superstar. He the American, me the Ivorian. So close, yet so far.

I ran into him in Los Angeles, at a pre-season party for Chelsea called 'Red Carpet'. They tend to organise big party events for clubs, to help them network and promote their image. Mine too.

Snoop Dogg showed up and of course I instantly recognised him. I went over to shake his hand and we were introduced. Then he clicked: 'Yeah, you're Drogba, that dude who plays for the Ivory Coast team and scores all those goals. You know, when I'm on the PlayStation I always pick you for my team.

You're my soccer guy!' We've stayed in touch ever since and I must be helping him to win a few games on the console . . . I hadn't realised the impact football has in the US. Kevin Garnett, this professional basketball player with the Boston Celtics, is crazy about it, he knows everything. We got on well, became friendly and keep in touch still.

I never thought that one day I'd get attention from people from the NBA, these big transatlantic stars. These were people I looked up to as giants and not just because of their height . . . Garnett has the most amazing track record, fame and an amazing aura. My world just got bigger.

Obviously sport isn't the only thing in my world, my only link to the outside. I really enjoyed speaking with Luc Besson for instance. I really admire him, beyond his talents as a film director and producer. His humanitarian side has helped raise the profile of Parisian suburbs. He's worked hard to instil a different vision of the estates, which I think is a fantastic scheme. I was also chosen to present the award for record of the year to Amadou & Mariam, the Malian duo, at the London Brixton Academy, for their album *Dimanche à Bamako* at the BBC Awards for World Music. Yet another honour, me all suited and booted – quite something.

I'm sometimes surprised by my popularity outside of Africa. It transcends borders. At home I have stacks of awards from all over, from the States for instance, like those diplomas people get from Dallas or Asia. They pile up, but I keep them all.

Gulf countries have taken me to their hearts. I was invited

to Dubai by Sheikh Mansour, who wanted to meet me. Geremi, my mate from Cameroon, had put us in touch.

His hospitality was amazing: the kind of stay and hotel one could only dream of. We'd stopped to look at this beautiful building which was under construction.

– Do you like it?

– Yes, it's absolutely beautiful!

– Then let me give you an apartment in there as a gift!

He just gave it to me on a whim – what a tremendous present! I couldn't believe it. I have this jeweller friend who lives in Switzerland, who insisted on leaving a mark of his talent on my wrist. Did he even know what a big watch fan I am?

I have forged ties and made contacts that will one day be able to help me when my footballing days are over. This is something that inspires me and opens up new perspectives. I thought this world was reserved for an elite, but this isn't always the case.

I've seen the other side of the coin, and the only reason I'm mentioning it now is to show that sometimes you need to truly go for what you want. Believe in yourself. Find your own way. Nothing had prepared me for this kind of existence. Of course, I'm making the most of it. The clothes, the trips, the cars . . . the ultimate footballer's toys. The parking area where we train looks like the garage of some luxury car dealer. I've bought a Ferrari, a Mercedes . . . My mother recently reminded me of what I used to tell her as a kid: 'When I'm famous, I'm going buy a Porsche 911.' At the time, just the words of a teenager, but now I've driven a bunch of cars and worked my way through all the different models: my wife's Golf 3, an Opel Zafira. As I moved up the ranks from transfer to transfer, I set myself challenges – 'If you do well here, you're getting yourself a nice present!' These were real conditions – I didn't want to fall into the trap of compulsive spending, but cars have never been my priority and have never made me score more goals.

I have always put my parents' wishes before mine. They brought me into the world, gave me the chance to come to France, and I am where I am thanks to them. My pleasure comes second to theirs.

My earnings allow me to help them. Yes, I make a lot of cash, but that's part of the business – I think I deserve it. Even if I'm one of England's best-paid players, I always set myself new targets. I don't envy anyone else, or if I do, it's in a positive and constructive way. This helps me progress to the next stage, but I never ask myself: why does this player have so much? I've never compared myself to others – I just don't think that way.

Of course, my life is much easier now. I hire private jets, so I can travel all over Europe in the space of just two or three hours. In terms of comfort and convenience, there's nothing like it. These are just added benefits, the icing on my cake – you can easily live without all that. I wasn't unhappy when I was younger, despite having so little.

When I think about how I used to pinch myself when I signed my first endorsements . . . At Guingamp, I didn't even have any. As I wore Nike, Cédric Bardon, Hakim Saci, Coco

Michel, my teammates gave me the number of Nicolas Piry, the guy who looked after the brand.

I rang him up, far from confident.

– Hi, my name is Didier Drogba, I'm a new player with Guingamp. Do you think you could send me some shoes, seeing as I wear Nike?

– You're not one of our players but I like your attitude. I'll give you two pairs. It's all that's left because everyone has taken the rest.

– No worries – thanks.

All I had to do was give them my shoe size. I was well pleased with myself, even without a contract. When I signed to Marseille, Nike and Adidas fought over me but Nike had the major advantage of knowing me, of having forged stronger ties, so I couldn't let them down.

At that time, Malamine Koné, this young Malian designer from Airness, got in touch with me. He wanted me and Steve Marlet to be the new faces of his Streetwear range. He liked my style. Djibril Cissé, his previous ambassador, had gone to Adidas. Cool. I signed for two years. Nike weren't very happy to see me dressed in Airness: Malamine Koné was starting to expand into all areas of sport, not just fashion.

I liked what his work did for my image in France and I owe him a lot, but I had to choose Nike, as their boots were the tools of my trade. Just before leaving him, I shot an ad – my first ever! Too bad it never made it to television because of my switch between sponsors – I was juggling and doing all these step-overs next to a panther! I wasn't so cocky then – I was a little tense even though the tamer stayed close to the cat. At one point, the beast got annoyed – I wouldn't have wanted to be its master. So we took a quick shot with the panther, and I hardly even stroked it.

They edited it to make the scene look more realistic. It was a great ad that hardly anybody got to see except me. After that, I got my first speaking role in a chocolate ad. I love getting away from the pitch. It changes my routine, plus I'm a real TV fan. 'As seen on TV': this phrase means something to me. It's fun to watch yourself – your friends call you up about it, and you never tire of it. Well, I don't get tired, anyway, of any of this. Everything happened so late in my career that I'm still loving every minute.

These days I can't even walk or drive around London without saying hi to people who recognise me. Same goes for Paris of course – it's my town. But what about Africa?

You wouldn't believe the madness that follows every move I make. I was really touched at my reception in Cameroon at the World Cup eliminatory in 2004. This appreciation amazes me. It's almost like love. In Madagascar, Burundi, Sudan . . . people want to touch me, to see me, talk to me.

In Côte d'Ivoire, it's even worse. I can't even go out in the street or wander around any more without causing mayhem. In June 2004, I even ended up fleeing Abidjan – I was inundated with invitations, lunch with such and such a minister . . . I took the first return flight. I wasn't ready to live out this kind of passion at that point, but it's easier now. I can't live without the Côte d'Ivoire, without breathing the air of my own continent. Maybe this is hard to understand from a European perspective. Ronaldo, Ronaldinho, Pelé, Maradona must face the same madness whenever they go home to South America – I know that Zidane does, in France and other places.

These days, I stick to the VIP lounge at the airport. There's no other way, no way to blend into a queue.

Whether I'm in a hotel lobby, in a restaurant, there's always someone who will come up to me and thank me, talk to me. Sometimes they're polite, sometimes more aggressive. But how could I turn them away? I don't always belong to myself any more.

I never push anyone away. People come to declare their love, to comfort me, sometimes even to chant to me. These people will always be there, they're lifetime fans. You mustn't be afraid of them; you have to listen to them. Of course, this demands a certain commitment. When I'm tired or not feeling good about things I have to keep myself in check, but it doesn't happen that often.

Ivorians have really wild imaginations. Some hairdressers offer the Drogba haircut, a lot of football tournaments promoting peace bear my name, some 'maquis' do too. They're sometimes called 'Le Chelsea' or 'Stamford Bridge'. There's even a beer which has been christened 'Drogba'! Don't go thinking that I've invested into a brewery. It's just that seeing the shape of the 75 cl or 1 litre bottle, young people or a (shrewd) manufacturer decided to give it that nickname. So even though it wasn't doing very well originally, the beer suddenly became a hit and now has the place of honour on every table! Some music bands have seized this opportunity. The Dream Team was the precursor. The first time I ever heard the chorus to their song was the night Côte d'Ivoire played Egypt in June 2005. I'd scored two goals and was feeling a bit emotional: I was becoming conscious of this emerging trend. Since then it's turned into a real goldmine: there's even something called the 'Drogbacité', a kind of dance inspired by my football moves.

Some of my team no longer want to go out with me, so in this respect the attention is embarrassing. We'll all be in a room and people will flock to me. I find this situation uncomfortable. Whenever people ask me for my autograph, I pass the sheet to my mates after I've signed it. It's tough when you cause jealousies and resentments without meaning to. I've stopped counting how many kisses, autographs and smiles I give out through the day. When I'm driving, I have to push people away crowding round the doors. It scares my children sometimes to see all those young people throwing themselves on the bonnet, holding on to the doors. I've left behind several wing mirrors at traffic lights! Sometimes it's best to actually jump the red lights . . . Once I even had to hide under a seat to leave this hotel in Abidjan which was surrounded by fans. There are so many anecdotes to tell: one disabled guy forced me to stop by threatening to throw himself under my car. I even heard that some parents wanted to call their children Didier-Drogba! This popularity affects my family too: my father, when people recognise him, can pass through police road blocks without any hassle. It does have its advantages . . .

When I hear people talk about me as a potential president of Côte d'Ivoire, it just amazes me.

I can understand how you can be a fan, but some people take it much too far. Saying that, they're always sincere and earnest, and I respect that. I'm touched by their attitude. I also ask myself whether this fame is about football or the work I do promoting peace in Côte d'Ivoire.

It isn't always easy for Lalla, my wife. When we go out to a club, despite my love of dancing I can't go near the dance floor without being immediately surrounded so I can't move an inch. Women don't exactly hold back either . . . Once, this girl threw herself on me from the top of some stairs: Lalla was almost hit by this unidentified flying object! Another one cornered me in the toilets of some nightclub. It doesn't put me off going out: it's in my nature.

I have to give back to the Côte d'Ivoire what it's given me. I've had wells dug in my parents' village, I asked for the school, the place where lives start to grow, to be refurbished . . . My only fear is to see this money being squandered, so I created my own charity with people who manage everything on site. I came up with the idea after visiting an orphanage – I wanted to make the most of my impact and my name. This foundation was set up to fight disease, to teach basic hygiene in order to help reduce health hazards.

I hope soon to be able to build a hospital too. These things matter to me.

I didn't make these investments for publicity or to make myself look good – that's not my style. There are so many people who like me that this passion stirs me up. I've seen people burst into tears when I walk past, while others stop me to tell me their troubles. How can this kind of thing not affect you? I get letters from children orphaned by the war that's rocking the Côte d'Ivoire. Terrible letters. I sometimes wonder how I'm going to manage to even play the next day . . . Not possible. These images are too strong, too compelling. I've been sent photos of people with third-degree burns, in unbearable agony. My cousins call me saying: 'My school has been shut down, I can't go there any more.' It was destroyed. School is basic. How can you let a place of knowledge perish, the place that builds tomorrow's adults?

Even if I'd been successful in a different field I'd still have this will to give, to help. I grew up with this sense of community. Whenever a meal was served at home, there'd be five or six of us eating from the same bowl. I was always taught to share, full stop. This idea is important in the Côte d'Ivoire and Africa as a whole.

My relationship with money isn't always easy. I can't just pay for everything either. I'll be the first to reach into my pocket but there are limits. When well-off people ask me for money, to me it's tantamount to extortion. Some people choose the easy way: they go up to players saying 'I have this project, I need 10 or 50 million CFA francs [15,000 or 76,000 euros].' I reckon you have to lend a hand without subsidising people completely. I've come to realise that constantly giving to your own friends doesn't help. I did it for a long time but I've now changed my approach.

It also takes pressure off me. I've just opened a clothing shop in London and employed relatives who are thereby able to become independent. I help them, it's true, but they definitely pay me back in kind. The main thing is not to be a football player or a minister but to be a man with values – to know how to hold a debate, give your opinion, share your feelings. I didn't have an extensive education but this has never been a social barrier. This may sound pretentious, but I feel I have more than enough intellect to take part in conversation. Even without graduating from high school, I've kept learning.

What can I say about being named a UN goodwill ambassador in early 2007? I am the third football player to be given this honour after Zidane and Ronaldo. The person in charge of the programme had asked who would be willing to represent the African continent for the UNDP and my name came up. That was that. Ronaldo, Zidane, Drogba.

This promotion is something I am so very proud of. It's a huge honour. As soon as I arrived in Geneva, at the UN headquarters, this building laden with symbolism and history, I thought of everything I had learned at school, post-war . . . It was quite emotional. It's an important moment in my life, as I have always felt a citizen of the world. Of the Côte d'Ivoire, of France, England, Mali, Senegal and elsewhere. United Nations – the concept fits me like a glove.

20

NEVER WITHOUT MY STAFF

In this book I've already mentioned the name of Pascal, without explaining his exact role. He was at my side on that sad evening when I left Marseille. My friend Pascal is never far away.

He's a bit like my shadow, there wherever I go, whether to the Ivory Coast or Ghana for the African Cup. If you come to my place there's a good chance you'll see him pop round for an hour. Pascal and I clicked immediately, and he became a close and loyal friend. He's a real Breton, full of character, and he keeps my feet on the ground . . .

He and Stéphane are the team that has supported me since leaving Guingamp. It was Florent Malouda, who was already using their services, who put us in contact. I often saw Flo after matches – he would recover faster than me. He suggested we hook up, and we've stayed together ever since. Stéphane is a sports physiotherapist specialising in fascia therapy, which is a technique that works on the body's fascia, its soft connective tissue. Each impact creates micro-contractions, and the more impacts you suffer, the more the muscle contracts. It becomes unable to bear further stress without negative effects. So you need to prepare your body for this exercise, like an expert in kung fu or boxing who gets used to taking blows.

Pascal has an academic background – his approach is scientific. During his studies he met a professor who had specialised for forty years in football research, and when he retired he passed down his knowledge and skills to Pascal. So I'm supported by two people coming at the job from different viewpoints – one in direct contact with the body, the other a specialist in the game.

This is the first time I've mentioned this collaboration, as early on people would bandy around words like 'sect', in particular with Eric Carrière, who uses Pascal and Stéphane. This stupid reasoning was what kept me quiet about working with them. Bizarre.

Once this caused problems for Carrière at Nantes. The staff of the Canaries didn't really understand what he was doing, and thought he was stepping on their toes. That was a totally wrong analysis, since our partnership never conflicted with their work. It wasn't about taking over someone's patch, but wanting to develop in our own way. Carrière, Malouda and I had been voted the best players in the French league, and this was down to more than luck.

A physiotherapist can't deal with twenty-one individuals in a row, and often gets stuck on the most pressing cases. What's more, not every player reacts in the same way. I'm one case; Florent Malouda or Carrière are different cases. Each of us needs to push himself to the max, try and exceed his limits.

At first I felt I was working flat out, but in the last six or seven matches of my season at Guingamp I started to hit another level. At that time I was only seeing Pascal, but I felt at ease, less on edge. Freed from the tensions I'd had. Then I went to see Stéphane: he concentrated on cranial rhythms to relax the body, help it recover more quickly.

So what exactly did we do to get things right?

Pascal assured me that I could push my potential further if only I made that extra bit of effort. He and Stéphane strove to develop my physical ability. Seeing quick results really helped. We watched videos, analysing games and tackles. We looked at what didn't work and tried to fix it. We went through everything: how to beat a defender by turning or dribbling, when to kick and when to dribble when you're one on one, what to do when the goalie came forward – is it better to pass him or to let him come at you?

So we had to learn to accept criticism to develop, reach the top of our game. Like a musician practising his scales I had to assess myself, work on the most minor faults. Over the years I used videos less and less – I didn't really need them any more, but they helped me to increase my know-how. These sessions

were almost like remedial classes at school. I was demanding –
the harder we worked, the happier I was. I had a craving to
learn, perhaps a hangover from my previous shortcomings and
my unusual career path.

Pascal really focuses on the scientific approach: he is
interested in perception, peripheral vision, central vision, the
type of visual signals you take into account when playing,
markers, speed, anticipating gaps . . .

All this may sound like double Dutch, but in fact the
concept is supremely simple. An example: you watch where an
opponent goes and analyse what you should have done to take
yourself out of his field of vision and pass unnoticed.
Sometimes all you have to do is slip into his blind spot before
shaking off your marker. 'Float like a butterfly, sting like a bee'
was the motto of the legendary Muhammad Ali. Always,
constantly think ahead. Anticipate your opponent's moves, the
way he uses the pitch. At this level of the game there's no room
for error.

You need to assess the situation before choosing the right
solution. I saw how Sonny Anderson was able to wander off to
one side, as if losing interest in the game, then score right
under the defender's nose. This part of the game seems simple,
but it takes training.

Even in front of the goal, I got used to visualising the
defenders' and goalie's moves. Sharpening my eyesight,
making every movement a reflex. I used to watch tapes of
famous strikers like Pauleta, the Portuguese star, who was a
delight to watch within the 18-yard line. A real presence,

always with great moves, great timing. And Trézéguet, with his amazing finishing. It used to annoy me hearing people criticising him all the time: take a good look at the position of his body, his feet, and you'll see why he's so effective . . .

We worked together on the pitch, especially at the beginning: ten or fifteen minutes of exercises, understanding how to use the space. Everything depends on that split-second advantage over your opposite number, vital at such a high level. It's often the difference between winning and losing a confrontation, winning and losing a match. Pascal's work was focused on the functioning of the brain, seeing how far I could think ahead, but obviously there was more to it than that.

We used to study videos for thirty minutes before hitting the pitch, or after matches. I've lost count of how many evenings we spent carefully watching, making precise analyses. Not to mention the time I spent warming up. All this came with a huge amount of physical effort. I spent at least an hour and a half warming up, strengthening muscles: I still keep it up almost every day – never quit, never think you've got it made.

This requires a serious personal investment. You need to know what you want. As I explained before, I found the knockabout style of the English premiership difficult at the beginning – the endless clashes and collisions were hard on my body. I spent many hours working with Pascal on this – the floor of my home must have really felt it! I had to get my body used to combat, strengthen my muscles. There was no question of taking it easy, forgetting the basics.

What's more, Pascal and Stéphane help me through

difficult times, especially when I am injured, and I have a fair bit of experience in that area . . .

So the aim is to improve myself to help the team, to adapt my style, the way I move in relation with my teammates, off and on the ball. This has nothing to do with the role of the trainer or the makeup of the starting eleven. I know what I owe them. And I've never had a trainer who didn't praise my commitment, which proves how this extra work, this personal investment benefits the team. To me that is vital.

Epilogue

RESPECT

I wanted to retrace the path that led me to my dreams. This need to share my story was born from the many requests I got. In both Africa and Europe, I've lost count of how many times I've been asked to tell my story. I wanted to put it down on paper, just to help out, to prove that you should never stop believing.

You probably gathered that I came across a lot of obstacles along the way, my body suffered but I hung in there. Maybe you didn't imagine so many doubts, uncertainties and hard times lurking behind this success . . . Those moments when you lose sight of your passion, when you think your world is collapsing. A career, mine at any rate, can sometimes hinge on almost nothing, on mere details. Without Marc

Westerloppe, would Le Mans have held on to me? What would have become of me if my parents hadn't chosen to send me to France? My life is so unreal now that it often does make me wonder. Most likely I'd have carried on studying, but would education have brought me this far? The story of my life is all about those meetings, changes in direction, hopes and sacrifices.

Anyway, I never turned from my original ambitions or changed my approach. I've always shown respect and I've always wanted to be respected in return. Of course that's easy to say now. But I've never accepted absolutely everything, no more at Le Mans than with Chelsea. The following scene is so symbolic. In the Sarthe region: it's the first time that I, the newbie, lie down on the massage table and suddenly David Fanzel, who was already a professional, shows up.

– Let me go first, I'm in a rush. What the hell are you doing here?

– I'm not going anywhere. If you've got something to say, find another way to say it. No way I'm giving in. If you'd asked me differently I would have said fine; give me the same respect I give you.

And that was it, he waited. It was just a matter of principle. Another time, at Le Mans, Stéphane Samson showed up from Caen. He was the star player who'd come to replace Dagui Bakari. He wanted my number 10 shirt and just went 'I'll have that one!'

I just smiled and said, 'Well you can't have it because it's taken!' But then, more seriously, 'And don't talk to me like that.'

He went and saw Alain Pascalou, the assistant, who came to me and insisted: 'Didier, you're still young. Sometimes you have to know when to back down.'

Me: 'All he had to do was ask nicely.'

This story got back to Westerloppe, who told me to drop it. I agreed and ended up wearing the number 21. But not without a fight. I've always operated this way, placing everyone on an equal footing. First and foremost, as I've often said in this book, a club is a family. And that doesn't just go for the players. I remember this discussion I had with Christophe Bouchet, the president of Marseille, before the UEFA Cup final against Valencia. I wanted the bonuses to be awarded to the whole team, on and off the field. A victory is earned by all of us together, from the cleaning lady to the striker. Don't go thinking this was tub-thumping; I've told you how the cooks at Le Mans helped me get back up off the ground and to smile again.

I'd actually been deeply affected by the death of a young Chelsea employee, Victoria Buchanan, who was hit by a bus on the way to our training area. Those people who help us out every day are wonderful. They do it out of love. This girl wasn't even thirty years old . . . This getting attached to people may be because I left Côte d'Ivoire at such a young age. I've overcome exile, moving, and I have an iron will, but I love to feel that human warmth, like I'm in a cocoon. I need to be able to lean on close bonds, to feel support around me. You can't get away from your past . . .

I've always wanted to look in the mirror without feeling like I wasn't being true to myself. I think I've managed to get there. I want my children, Kévin, Isaac and Iman to follow the same path; I want them to be respectful and to have a lot to give from a human point of view. Who can I become in the future? I wonder about that sometimes, but I intend to carry on with this beautiful balloon journey for a good while longer. I'm not setting myself an age limit. I'd obviously like to see other countries, like Italy and Spain, but after that it'll be time to pack it in. I'm not set on staying in football. I sometimes think I might like to leave, but it never takes long before my love for it just catches up with me. The things I've experienced recently make me want to support those who want to change this sport's image.

Africa brings me a lot in terms of fame and I'm thinking about the best ways to give back what I get. Right now I'm just not quite sure how, but I definitely don't see myself in politics.

In London, in August 2007, I met George Weah, unsuccessful candidate for the presidency of Liberia. I was overwhelmed at the thought that my childhood hero was asking to see me and to have one of my shirts. That night in London he told me of his struggle, about the relations between Liberia, Burkina Faso and Côte d'Ivoire, confided about the grievous effect of his country's civil war years. I listened to him like you'd listen to a teacher, impressed. But I don't feel like I could get into it, not for now anyway.

*

You may not have seen the last of the Drogba family though. Freddy, one of my younger brothers, is now with Le Mans and he's a champion in the making. As a child, all he dreamed of was football. He'd play in any weather, whether it snowed or rained and when it was cold: nothing put him off. He reminds me of another Drogba . . . I haven't made much mention of these people who are so dear to me, just because we didn't get a chance to grow up together. My moving away from Africa and my professional obligations have distanced us physically, but we're still very close in our hearts. Family's sacred to me.

Freddy definitely has real talent; so does Isaac. As a baby, he'd sleep with his football and would cry when it was taken away from him. Some start . . . His passion is growing with the years that pass; he always has a ball close by and he likes to challenge me. It would be beautiful to see him make it. Bizarrely enough, in every team I've ever played in, he's always had a favourite player and it was never his dad. But if he becomes a pro, there's no doubt that I'll be his number one fan, I can guarantee him that . . .

INDEX